LIFE
PRESERVERS

God's promises for troubled times

BOB RUSSELL

STANDARD
PUBLISHING
Cincinnati, Ohio

Library of Congress Cataloging-in-Publication Data

Life preservers : God's promises for troubled times / Bob Russell.
    p.   cm.
  Includes bibliographical references.
  ISBN 0-7847-0573-9
  1. God—Promises.   2. God—Promises—Biblical teaching.
3. Christian life.
BT180.P7L54   1997   96-33549
231.7—dc20   CIP

Cover design by SCHULTZWARD.

The Standard Publishing Company, Cincinnati, Ohio.
A division of Standex International Corporation

© 1997 by The Living Word, Inc.
All rights reserved.
Printed in the United States of America.

04   03   02   01   00   99   98   97   5   4   3   2   1

CONTENTS

GOD KEEPS HIS PROMISE

In 1989 a devastating earthquake flattened the country of Armenia, killing over thirty thousand people in less than four minutes. In the midst of the confusion that followed, a father left his wife securely at home and rushed to his son's school, hoping for the best but fearing the worst. When he arrived, he discovered to his horror that the school building had been flattened.

While surveying the rubble he remembered the promise he had often made to his young son: "No matter what, I'll always be there for you!" The situation looked hopeless, but he could not take his mind off that promise. He remembered that his son's classroom was in the back right corner of the building. He rushed there and started digging through the rubble. Other grieving parents arrived, crying for their children. Some tried to pull the man off the rubble saying, "It's too late! They're dead. You can't help!" Even a police officer told him to go home.

Courageously he proceeded alone because he needed to know for himself whether his boy was dead or alive. He dug for eight hours, then twelve, then twenty-four, then thirty-six hours. Finally, in the thirty-eighth hour he pulled back a boulder and heard his son's voice. He screamed his son's name, "Armand!"

A voice answered him, "Dad? It's me, Dad!" Then the boy added these priceless words: "I told the other kids not to worry. I told them that if you were alive, you'd save me and when you saved me, they'd be saved. You promised, 'No matter what I'll always be there for you.' You did it, Dad!"

"I promise." In a world where most people would rather do what they feel like doing than keep their word, that phrase may seem pretty meaningless—unless the promise comes from a loving father.

We have a perfect heavenly Father. Is there anyone on earth as loving and unselfish as God? Does anyone care more about you than He does? Is there anyone who is more true to His word? Is there anyone who has sacrificed more for you? Absolutely not. When God makes a promise, you can believe He will do what He says, no matter what.

God has made many promises to you, especially promises for you to remember in times of trouble or hardship. He knew you would endure your share of earthquakes in this world, and God wanted you to be comforted during difficult times. This book examines those promises, which were first recorded in His love letter to you called the Bible.

I hope you are able to use this book as a reference tool after you have read it through the first time. I hope you'll remember the topics, and when you're going through tough times—times of grief, fear, doubt, worry, financial stress, or even the difficulties and stresses that come from prosperous times—you will get it back out and look for the chapters that deal with those topics. When those times of difficulty come, get this book back off the shelf. Skim through and find the verses I've quoted that tell you exactly what God has promised you. Read the stories again of people like you who have relied on the promises of God in their troubled times, and have discovered the joy of knowing Someone loves you enough to keep His Word. May God's Word remain true in your life through your troubled times.

"Praise be to the Lord, who has given rest to his people Israel just as he promised. Not one word has failed of all the good promises he gave through his servant Moses."

1 Kings 8:56

Your love, O Lord, reaches to the heavens,
your faithfulness to the skies. *Psalm 36:5*

God, who has called you into fellowship with his Son Jesus Christ our Lord, is faithful. *1 Corinthians 1:9*

The Lord is not slow in keeping his promise. *2 Peter 3:9*

If we are faithless,
he will remain faithful,
for he cannot disown himself. *2 Timothy 2:13*

The one who calls you is faithful and he will do it.

1 Thessalonians 5:24

IN TIMES OF FEAR

Joshua 5, 6

Last summer I had the most terrifying experience of my life. My wife, Judy, who is in her early fifties, suffered a stroke. I was called out of a meeting and a friend rushed me to the hospital. I had no idea how serious her situation was until I got there. My heart raced as I prayed that God would spare her.

When I arrived at the hospital, Judy was sitting up in bed, and I was so grateful that everything appeared to be fine. We were thankful that she was experiencing only mild paralysis in her left arm, and the doctor's prognosis was that all feeling would return in a short period of time. She would need to spend a few days in the hospital for some tests, but what a relief that things were not worse!

Then during her first night in the hospital, Judy experienced a severe facial seizure. She cried out for help as her pretty face was yanked and twisted in every direction for about thirty seconds. Not knowing what was happening, we both assumed she was having a second massive stroke.

I have never been so terrified nor felt so helpless. A friend of mine who is a missionary in Africa told me later that he had been gored by a buffalo, mauled by a lion, and had battled malaria, but he said, "The most terrified I've ever been was when my wife was sick and I couldn't help her."

My wife's seizures were repeated every half hour until they were eventually controlled with medication. We are so thankful to God that at the time I am writing this, she has had almost total recovery with no recurrence of the seizures.

What terrifies you? We are born with only two fears: the fear of falling and the fear of loud noises. All other fears are learned or acquired, primarily from the adversary, Satan. Yet we learn at an early age to be afraid of many things. I heard of one little boy who was terrified of the dark. His mother said, "Honey, don't be afraid. We're right next door. And remember God is with you in your room."

The boy reluctantly tiptoed back into his room and slowly cracked open the door. He whispered, "God, if You're in here, don't You dare move or You'll scare me to death!"

When we reach adulthood, our fears become more sophisticated. If they are not conquered, our fears can hinder our relationships with God and others. Fear can control and enslave us. Carol Kent has written an excellent book, *Tame Your Fears,* in which she lists some of the most enslaving fears that most people face: paralyzing phobias, potential disasters, losing control, revealing who I really am, disappointing people, and being rejected (Carol Kent, *Tame Your Fears,* NavPress, 1993, pp. 17-22).

PARALYZING PHOBIAS

One of my favorite cartoon scenes is in "Charlie Brown's Christmas Special," when Lucy, the "psychiatrist," is trying to diagnose Charlie Brown's emotional problems. Assuming that Charlie Brown's problem is fear, she lists several popular "phobias" in an effort to determine which one he has. Finally she says, "Charlie Brown, maybe you have panophobia—the fear of everything."

Charlie Brown blurts out, "That's it!"

While most of us do not have panophobia, we could name one phobia that might enslave us on occasion. Maybe you have acrophobia (fear of heights), claustrophobia (fear of closed-in spaces), hydrophobia (fear of water), xenophobia (fear of strangers), or even triskaidekaphobia (fear of the number thirteen)! Any such phobia can be paralyzing.

FEAR OF POTENTIAL DISASTERS

When your spouse is fifteen minutes late, do you begin planning the funeral? Are you constantly afraid of losing your job? Are you a Weather Channel junkie, afraid of what disaster may come next? Do you check the doors every night numerous times to make sure they're locked, bolted, and barred? You may have had a bad experience in the past that you feel legitimizes your fears, but those fears can still be paralyzing and ungodly.

FEAR OF LOSING CONTROL

Everyone knows a perfectionist. His desk is always paper free; her house is immaculate; their kids are perfect. Sometimes that perfectionist is masking a fear of losing control. Others don't do such a good job of masking their fear. They work hard to maintain control of everything. They run the house; they control every decision; they question you if you don't check with them before picking out your clothes or choosing a meal or planning an evening. They often panic at the thought of their kids growing up. They will avoid all group settings where they are not the dominant party.

FEAR OF REVEALING WHO I REALLY AM

America is a great nation. There is no place in the world where it is easier to break from your past or to be successful despite your upbringing. Add to that the forgiveness the church offers, and being a Christian in America can be liberating. But our past may still haunt us. A person will sometimes tell me he would rather not talk about anything that happened "B.C.," meaning before Christ came into his life. A lot of people don't want others to know too much about their past. That's normal, but it can be taken to extremes. You can constantly worry that people will find out who you really are. You can live in fear of what others would think if they knew the truth.

FEAR OF DISAPPOINTING PEOPLE

Women have stayed for years in abusive relationships because they are afraid of disappointing their parents or Christian friends. Children have chosen occupations they hated, and have married people they didn't like, to please their parents or uphold the family name rather than disappoint someone. You might know a person who refuses to repent of his sin, because to confess and change his ways would mean disappointing a lot of people who thought they knew him well.

FEAR OF BEING REJECTED

A spouse or a parent can hold you in bondage by threatening to abandon you if you don't live up to certain expectations. Maybe you have even experienced such rejection. Your parents divorced or your mate left unexpectedly, leaving you feeling guilty and responsible even if you weren't. If you are not careful, you can enter every new relationship expecting to be rejected unless you are perfect. Such devastating fear can hold you in emotional bondage unless it is overcome.

God does not want you to be afraid. I'm not referring to the "fear of God" that the Bible calls as a good thing, or the "self-preserving fear" that gives us the good sense not to play in the street or go too near the edge of a cliff. I mean that God does not want you to be enslaved to the kinds of fears I have listed.

In Jesus' parable of the talents, the man given one talent buried his talent in the ground because he was afraid of what might happen if he took a risk. Jesus condemned the man for allowing an ungodly fear of rejection to overtake him, steal his courage and make him lazy (see Matthew 25). To make a decision or to take an action based on that kind of fear is disobedience to God. He has commanded us in His Word to trust in Him and not be afraid. To do otherwise is to disobey and show a lack of faith in God's promises. God commands us:

> *Do not let your hearts be troubled and do not be afraid.*
>
> *John 14:27*

Fear not, for I have redeemed you;
  I have summoned you by name; you are mine.
When you pass through the waters,
  I will be with you;
and when you pass through the rivers,
  they will not sweep over you.
When you walk through the fire,
  you will not be burned;
  the flames will not set you ablaze.
For I am the Lord, your God,
  the Holy One of Israel, your Savior.   *Isaiah 43:1-3.*

In her book, Carol Kent explains that God gave us the emotion of fear as a positive motivator. It keeps us alert, gives us adrenaline and gives us a sense of challenge about life. But God does not want us to be afraid—to allow our fears to motivate us to inaction or wrong action. Rather than becoming slaves to fear, we must learn to "tame" our fears, channeling them correctly by focusing on God's promise to be with us through those times.

For you did not receive a spirit that makes you a slave again to fear, but you received the Spirit of sonship. And by him we cry, "Abba, Father."   Romans 8:15

JOSHUA'S REASONS TO BE AFRAID

The Israelite leader Joshua is an example of a man who focused on the promises of God and overcame his fears. In the first chapter of the book of Joshua, the Lord came to him and said:

"Moses my servant is dead. Now then, you and all these people, get ready to cross the Jordan River into the land I am about to give to them—to the Israelites."   Joshua 1:2

Three times in the first chapter, God commanded Joshua to be strong and very courageous (Joshua 1:6, 7, 9). God knew Joshua would need lots of encouragement, because he had plenty of reasons to be afraid.

HE WAS FOLLOWING A LEGEND

Joshua was following a legend. Moses had led the people of Israel for forty years. An entire generation of Israelites had died in the wilderness. The present group had known no other leader than Moses. Moses had rescued them from Egypt, had crossed the Red Sea, had brought them the Ten Commandments. Moses had been their judge and their spiritual leader. Moses had walked and talked with God. Would the people be willing to follow Joshua as they had Moses?

It is difficult to follow a legend. Ask Gene Bartow, who

resigned after just two years as head basketball coach at UCLA even though the team had two winning seasons. The pressure from the media and fans was oppressive. His record would have been acceptable anyplace else, but he was following the legendary John Wooden, who had won ten national championships. I'm sure the pressure people put on Joshua to be as great a leader as Moses was oppressive at times.

HE HAD WITNESSED A PREVIOUS FAILURE

Forty years earlier the Israelites had been in the same situation. Instead of being strong and courageous, they got cold feet. When they should have been focusing on the faithfulness of God's promises, they focused on the size of the enemy. Joshua had been there. He was one of only two men who believed in the power of God and trusted the Lord to give them victory. As a result, Joshua and his faithful friend, Caleb, were the only two from his generation God allowed to live long enough to enter the promised land. Would this younger generation get cold feet like their parents had?

Sometimes experience can be a detriment. We know the dangers that lie ahead. That's why young people are often bolder than we who have experienced life's successes and failures. We tend to be cynical, predicting they will be more humble after they've failed a few times. "Ignorance is bliss," we say.

Joshua was not ignorant. He knew the people were capable of backing out on him at the last minute, especially after they saw the size of their formidable enemies.

THE ENEMY FORCES WERE INTIMIDATING

Joshua and Caleb were the only ones who had witnessed what their enemies were really like. They had chosen to focus on the wonders of the land that would someday be theirs, but in the back of their minds they knew that the other ten spies were right: the cities *were* well fortified and the people *were* like giants. Joshua could be sure that things had not changed much in the forty years since their undercover expedition.

HE HAD NOT PERFORMED MIRACLES

In the past, whenever they encountered difficulty, it had been the rod of Moses that displayed miraculous powers. God had worked through Moses. Would God work through Joshua as well? What if they came to the Jordan River and the rod didn't work? Did he have the faith in God he needed? Did God truly have confidence in him as the chosen leader?

THEY HAD LITTLE BATTLE EXPERIENCE

Though there had been a few skirmishes with enemy clans in the desert, the Israelites were not battle hardened. They would be fighting against Canaanites who were experienced warriors. Would there be casualties? Most certainly. Joshua would have to face the mothers and wives of those who died in battle.

Someone said, "Experience is a tough teacher. It gives the test first and the lesson afterward." Would the Israelite armies have to go to the "school of hard knocks" before they were victorious?

GOD'S PROMISES IN TIMES OF FEAR

You can see why God had to repeat three times the challenge to Joshua to "be strong and courageous." God knew Joshua faced temptations to be weak and cowardly.

But God did not just command Joshua to be courageous. He gave him this great promise:

No one will be able to stand up against you all the days of
your life. As I was with Moses, so I will be with you; I will
never leave you nor forsake you.   Joshua 1:5

God has issued every believer the same promise—that
He will always be with us—and the same challenge to be
strong and courageous.

"So do not fear, for I am with you;
  do not be dismayed, for I am your God.
I will strengthen you and help you;
  I will uphold you with my righteous right hand."
                                        Isaiah 41:10

It's not easy to take someone at his word. Promises can
be broken. That's why we have contracts, courts, and a
penal system. We want some reassurance that people will
keep their promises. God has never broken a promise
and will never break one, because it is impossible for God
to lie (Titus 1:2). He hasn't given us a signed contract because His Word is proof enough. But God graciously
gives us reassurances, as He did Joshua, that He will keep
His promises.

THROUGH THE TESTIMONY OF OTHERS

God sent Joshua reassurance of His presence from an
unlikely source—a Canaanite prostitute named Rahab.
After providing a hiding place for the spies sent to Jericho, risking her own life in the process, she said to them:

"I know that the Lord has given this land to you and that a
great fear of you has fallen on us, so that all who live in this
country are melting in fear because of you. We have heard
how the Lord dried up the water of the Red Sea for you when
you came out of Egypt, and what you did to Sihon and Og,
the two kings of the Amorites east of the Jordan, whom you
completely destroyed. When we heard of it, our hearts melted

and everyone's courage failed because of you, for the Lord your God is God in heaven above and on earth below."
                                                              Joshua 2:9-11

A once-popular talk show host recently blamed Christians who "have a Messiah complex" and "talk to God every day" for the failure of some afternoon talk shows. The host, whose shows have fizzled lately in popularity, criticized believers for pressuring advertisers into dropping support of television programs that carry objectionable content.

The host's criticism of Christians was really a backhanded compliment of the ability of believers to make a difference. When even those in the world are fearfully testifying to the power of God, we should be encouraged to stand by our convictions. Rahab said, "A great fear of you has fallen on us" (Joshua 2:9), and Joshua was encouraged. God was reassuring him that "the one who is in you is greater than the one who is in the world" (1 John 4:4).

Rahab made the spies promise to spare her life and the lives of her family members in exchange for her hiding place. They agreed to do so. Later, when the city of Jericho was destroyed, the spies remembered Rahab and saved her family as they had promised.

THROUGH THE SUPPORT OF GODLY LEADERS

Joshua said to the priests, "Take up the ark of the covenant and pass on ahead of the people." So they took it up and went ahead of them.   Joshua 3:6

What a confidence boost it must have been to Joshua when the priests were willing to follow his lead! They not only supported Joshua but they themselves led the people through the Jordan River and into battle against Jericho. It took courage for the priests to walk into the

Jordan River at flood stage carrying the ark of the covenant, but those righteous men were being led by God to do what Joshua had commanded. When you see others, especially godly men and women whom you respect, taking courageous steps to be obedient to God, it is reassuring.

The apostle Paul was thrown into jail for preaching the gospel, but he knew his persecution would result in others overcoming their fear of arrest. He wrote:

> *Now I want you to know, brothers, that what has happened to me has really served to advance the gospel. As a result, it has become clear throughout the whole palace guard and to everyone else that I am in chains for Christ. Because of my chains, most of the brothers in the Lord have been encouraged to speak the word of God more courageously and fearlessly.*
>
> Philippians 1:12-14

Thousands of Christians have been inspired to be more faithful, outspoken and courageous because of the example of godly leaders. In the Old Testament, Joshua stood firm against intimidating enemy forces; David faced a giant; Daniel refused to be intimidated by the lions' den. In the New Testament, Jesus and many of the apostles courageously faced suffering and death out of obedience to God. The eleventh chapter of Hebrews records the stories of many biblical heroes who faced their fears with courage and faithfulness. Even today, in our own country, people like Dr. James Dobson and Charles Colson boldly speak the truth through much opposition, inspiring others to do the same.

THROUGH UNEXPLAINABLE CIRCUMSTANCES
Now the Jordan is at flood stage all during harvest. Yet as soon as the priests who carried the ark reached the Jordan and their feet touched the water's edge, the water from up-

stream stopped flowing. It piled up in a heap a great distance away, at a town called Adam in the vicinity of Zarethan, while the water flowing down to the Sea of Arabah (the Salt Sea) was completely cut off. So the people crossed over opposite Jericho. Joshua 3:15, 16

Joshua knew the moment the priests' feet touched the Jordan River that God was truly with them. When we are willing to step out into the deep, God sometimes does miraculous or unexplainable things through us to reassure us of His presence.

In 1993, our church leaders voted to launch out into a building program. Our goal was to raise $26 million, above our regular offerings, over a three-year period of time. Experts told us that it was the largest goal of any church in history. We were convinced that the goal was so big, if God wasn't in it, we would fail.

Our church members were forced to evaluate their priorities, pray for guidance, and trust in God. One single mother of three teenagers testified that she and her children had decided to cancel their cable television for the next three years so they could donate the twenty-five dollars per month to the building fund. Other members sold cars, canceled vacations or cashed in their retirement plans so they could give. Some even took part-time jobs to earn extra money for the project. Those testimonies inspired others to sacrifice so they could give as generously as possible.

When the total was announced, the church had not pledged $26 million, but over $30 million! The "experts" who had said our goal was too big were stunned. We had one explanation: God was at work among us. We had no reason to fear.

In my thirty years of ministry, I have seen people healed of inoperable cancer, romance rekindled in dead marriages, hard hearts softened, babies born that were intended to be aborted, and souls saved against tremendous odds. I have seen innumerable examples of unexplainable circumstances, which can only be credited to the presence of God. Such events reassure us and strengthen our faith in times of fear.

For God did not give us a spirit of timidity, but a spirit of power, of love and of self-discipline.   *2 Timothy 1:7*

When you are afraid, look for God's reassurances through the testimony of others, the support of godly leaders and the occurrence of unexplainable circumstances. If you believe God's promises are true, you have no reason to fear.

Do you face a constant temptation to be afraid of something? Do you fear losing a loved one, aging, financial insecurity, being mugged, losing your job, a broken marriage, dying? Maybe you know God has called you to do something that frightens you—break a sinful habit, confront a wayward friend, heal a broken relationship, start a family, or take a new job. Remember that God allows you to experience fear so that you might learn to depend on His presence. Courage is not the absence of fear, but action in spite of fear. Be obedient. Seek the reassurance of other believers. Have faith in God's promises and not your own power. Conquer your fears with God's help. He has promised to be with you always. Remember His reassuring words to you. Be strong and courageous, for the Lord our God is with you!

Have no fear of sudden disaster
*   or of the ruin that overtakes the wicked,*
for the Lord will be your confidence
*   and will keep your foot from being snared.*
                                        Proverbs 3:25, 26

Even though I walk
    through the valley of the shadow of death,
I will fear no evil,
    for you are with me;
your rod and your staff,
    they comfort me.   Psalm 23:4, 5

The Lord is my light and my salvation—
    whom shall I fear?
The Lord is the stronghold of my life—
    of whom shall I be afraid?   Psalm 27:1

There is no fear in love. But perfect love drives out fear, because fear has to do with punishment. The one who fears is not made perfect in love.   1 John 4:18

So we say with confidence,
    "The Lord is my helper; I will not be afraid.
    What can man do to me?"   Hebrews 13:6

IN TIMES OF DOUBT

Judges 6, 7

Napoleon used to inspire his men by telling them about his most loyal soldier, a one-armed man who, in the heat of battle, lost his only arm. The man refused to quit and continued fighting until he had won the battle! One astute observer later described the incident as a story that was just too good to check out!

Some people see the Bible that way. It is such a good story that no one wants to discredit it, but too fanciful to really believe. Mark Twain once said that faith is "believing in something you know ain't so." But if you have integrity, it is impossible for you to say something is true if you know it is not true. Therefore, you have probably wrestled with the great stories of the Scriptures and asked yourself, "Are these things really true?" At times faith may come easy to you, and you say, "I know the Word of God is true." At other times you may feel a sense of doubt.

I heard a preacher explain that there are three ways we can approach God: belief, doubt, and unbelief. Belief and unbelief are choices, but doubt is an honest expression of emotion. It is possible to feel doubt even when you want to believe.

The Bible makes a clear distinction between the person

who is an unbeliever and the person who has occasional doubts during difficult times in life. Psalm 14:1 condemns the atheist as a fool, "The fool says in his heart, 'There is no God.'" Yet Jesus, while He often bemoaned the lack of faith of His disciples, was patient with them and continually tried to strengthen their faith. He did not condemn them for their occasional doubting.

Many of those who saw Jesus face to face, who witnessed His miracles, who heard His teaching and who knew He was the Messiah, had serious doubts when things got tough. When Peter saw Jesus walking on the water, he was amazed and asked if he, too, might walk on water. Jesus beckoned Peter to come. After Peter took a couple of bold steps on the water, his faith wavered and he began to sink.

"Immediately Jesus reached out His hand and caught him. 'You of little faith,' he said, 'why did you doubt?'" (Matthew 14:31). Peter had very serious lapses of faith even though Jesus was right there with him. But Jesus was patient with him, and Peter eventually became one of the boldest, most faithful heroes of the early church.

If Peter and the other disciples struggled with doubt, it should not surprise us when we have similar struggles today. We must remember, however, that faith is a mark of maturity while doubt is a sign of immaturity. Some Christians think they are somehow wiser or smarter if they "doubt" the supernatural events of the Bible. There is a difference between the occasional lapses of faith that we all experience and the cynicism of some liberal theologians. James warned us of the dangers of doubting, "He who doubts is like a wave of the sea, blown and tossed by the wind. That man should not think he will receive anything from the Lord; he is a double-minded man, unstable in all he does" (James 1:6, 7).

Yet Jude 22 commands, "Be merciful to those who

doubt." Since the Christian life is dependent upon faith in what is unseen, many will struggle with occasional doubts. Though we hope to overcome those doubts as we mature in Christ, it is comforting to read in Scripture God's promises to His servants who experienced the same struggles with doubt.

There was one such servant in the Old Testament with whom God was extraordinarily patient. His name was Gideon. We first read about Gideon in Judges 6. Because of the Israelites' disobedience, God had allowed a foreign army, the Midianites, to overtake the land of Israel. Many of the Hebrew people had fled to the mountains or were hiding in caves. Gideon was hiding in a wine cellar when an angel appeared to him.

GIDEON'S DOUBTS

When the angel of the Lord appeared to Gideon, he said, "The Lord is with you, mighty warrior."   Judges 6:12

Even though the words had come from an angel of God, Gideon didn't believe them. He doubted.

"But sir," Gideon replied, "if the Lord is with us, why has all this happened to us? Where are all his wonders that our fathers told us about when they said, 'Did not the Lord bring us up out of Egypt?' But now the Lord has abandoned us and put us into the hand of Midian."

The Lord turned to him and said, "Go in the strength you have and save Israel out of Midian's hand. Am I not sending you?"   Judges 6:13, 14

HE DOUBTED GOD'S CHOICE

"But Lord," Gideon asked, "how can I save Israel? My clan is the weakest in Manasseh, and I am the least in my family."   Judges 6:15

Gideon didn't have confidence in God's choice of leadership, namely, Gideon himself. The world grants leadership to the people who are the smartest, the most charismatic or the most attractive. We tend to think God is going to do the same thing. "Surely God would not call me to do something like that," we rationalize. Since others are more talented than we are, we want to think God is going to call them instead of us. Gideon complained that his family was the dullest, weakest bunch of people in all of Israel. Nobody would follow a son of Joash the Abiezrite. And besides, even in his family there were other siblings who could do the job much better than he. But God often uses the weak things of this world to shame the strong. He often calls the least likely person to become a leader in His kingdom.

Moses had tried to make the same claims of inadequacy many years earlier. God came to Moses in a burning bush and told him he had been chosen to lead the Israelites out of Egypt. Three times God was patient with him while Moses complained. He told God he didn't see himself as a capable leader. God assured him that he was. Then he tried to convince God no one would believe him, so God gave him miracles he could perform to prove he was from God. Moses persisted, claiming that such a leader should be an eloquent speaker, which he was not. God said He would convince Moses' brother Aaron, a great orator, to help. Finally Moses gave up on all of his excuses and simply said to God, "O Lord, please send someone else to do it" (Exodus 4:13).

But the Bible says that God's anger burned against Moses, and He commanded him to be obedient to His call. If God calls you, He believes you are capable of accomplishing the task. He may be patient with your self doubt for a while, but He expects you to obey the call. You might doubt God's choice, but God says to us, "Not

by might, nor by power, but by my Spirit" (Zechariah 4:6).
Jesus said:

*"Have faith in God. . . . I tell you the truth, if anyone says to
this mountain, 'Go, throw yourself into the sea,' and does not
doubt in his heart but believes that what he says will happen,
it will be done for him. Therefore I tell you, whatever you ask
for in prayer, believe that you have received it, and it will be
yours."* Mark 11:22-24

HE DOUBTED GOD'S LEADING
*Gideon replied, "If now I have found favor in your eyes, give
me a sign that it is really you talking to me."* Judges 6:17

After Gideon was sure he understood the command,
he began to question whether it really came from God.
"OK, God, I get the message . . . but how can I be sure
this message is really from You?"

Have you ever found yourself doing that? God probably hasn't spoken to you in an audible voice as He did to
Gideon. Today we rely on His written Word and the
prompting of the Holy Spirit. Therefore, it's even more
tempting for us to doubt His guidance. How do I know
God is leading me to this decision? What if I just want to
do it for my own ego? How do I know this really comes
from God?

Gideon asked God for a miraculous sign. He prepared
an offering for the Lord and brought it to the angel. The
angel told Gideon to place the meat and bread on a rock,
which Gideon did.

*With the tip of the staff that was in his hand, the angel of
the Lord touched the meat and the unleavened bread. Fire
flared from the rock, consuming the meat and the bread. And
the angel of the Lord disappeared.* Judges 6:21

Gideon was obviously scared. "I have seen the angel of

the Lord face-to-face!" he cried. But the Lord spoke to him again, assuring him that he had nothing to fear. "Peace!" God said. "Do not be afraid. You are not going to die" (Judges 6:23). In other words, calm down, Gideon! God is in control!

You would think such a dramatic sign would instill in Gideon confidence that he was indeed doing the Lord's will. But he was still unsure. There were a couple of things that happened to Gideon that made his confidence waver.

First, he received criticism from the people he was supposed to lead. God had commanded Gideon to tear down the Asherah pole (an altar to the false god Baal) that his father had built for the town. It would be like God telling someone today to set fire to the most popular X-rated theater in town. Gideon did what God had commanded, and the next day the whole town tried to kill him! His father had to come save him from the mob. That would tend to shake your faith!

Second, Gideon received a following. The Spirit of the Lord came upon Gideon, and he blew a trumpet, summoning the Abiezrites to follow him (Judges 6:34). And they did follow! You might think this would give Gideon a confidence boost. But just the opposite sometimes happens. When you realize that people are following you, it can be intimidating. What if I lead them in the wrong direction? What if they start following me, and then find out I'm really not that smart, or that I make mistakes, too? What if I can't measure up?

Because some were criticizing and others were following, Gideon began second-guessing God's sign. He asked for another miracle! He took a sheep's fleece and laid it on the threshing floor, then said, "Lord, if you really want me to do this, tonight when you let the dew fall, cover the sheep's fleece with dew and leave the ground dry" (Judges 6:36, 37, my paraphrase).

People often say, "I'm laying out a fleece regarding this decision," referring to Gideon's test of God. I've heard people credit God for His supposed answer to their "fleece" when I wasn't sure God wanted the credit! One woman said she was praying about whether she should take a trip to Hawaii, and she asked God for some sign. She woke up the next morning at 7:47 and took that at a sign that she was to take a 747 jet to Hawaii!

God answered Gideon's prayer, and the next morning Gideon found the fleece soaked with dew and the ground bone dry. But Gideon still doubted. He reversed the request just to be double sure.

Then Gideon said to God, "Do not be angry with me. Let me make just one more request. Allow me one more test with the fleece. This time make the fleece dry and the ground covered with dew." That night God did so. Only the fleece was dry; all the ground was covered with dew. Judges 6:39, 40

God patiently answered his second request as well. Gideon woke up and found the fleece dry, while the ground was soaked with the morning dew. Gideon finally believed, for a while, that it was God who was leading him.

HE DOUBTED GOD'S METHOD

Gideon gathered thirty-two thousand men to fight the Midianites. But God was concerned that the Israelites would think it was their own strength that defeated the Midianites, so He commanded Gideon to send all but three hundred of the men home. The Lord told Gideon He would conquer the Midianites with the remaining three hundred men! But God knew Gideon would again have his doubts.

During that night the Lord said to Gideon, "Get up, go down against the camp, because I am going to give it into your hands. If you are afraid to attack, go down to the camp with your servant Purah and listen to what they are saying. Afterward, you will be encouraged to attack the camp."

Judges 7:9-11

God said, "Gideon, if you're still scared, sneak down and eavesdrop on the conversations in the enemy camp." We know Gideon was afraid, because he and his servant did sneak down during the night to the Midianite camp. There he saw a sight that made him even more afraid:

The Midianites, the Amalekites and all the other eastern peoples had settled in the valley, thick as locusts. Their camels could no more be counted than the sand on the seashore.

Judges 7:12

Gideon discovered he would be greatly outnumbered. How could three hundred men fight that many people?

We find ourselves doubting God's methods today just as Gideon did. We think, How could preaching save this generation? Nobody uses the lecture method anymore. And how can you expect to reach teens and adults in this culture if you tell them all the things they "can't" do? You have to relax a little in this era. Or we wonder, How can you expect to teach your child self-esteem if you spank him? That is not the popular method. Or we question, Do you really think you can give away ten percent of your income and make it in today's economy?

But God was again patient with Gideon, and showed him that Israel would have the victory. Gideon and his servant sneaked closer to the camp. They arrived just as a Midianite was telling a friend his dream.

"I had a dream," he was saying. "A round loaf of barley bread came tumbling into the Midianite camp. It struck the

tent with such force that the tent overturned and collapsed."

His friend responded, "This can be nothing other than the sword of Gideon son of Joash, the Israelite. God has given the Midianites and the whole camp into his hands."

Judges 7:13, 14

When he realized God had instilled fear in the hearts of the enemy, Gideon finally believed in God's method and led his three hundred men against the Midianites. In the middle of the night, they surrounded the camp. Each of the three hundred men had a horn, a torch and an empty jar. At the signal, they all blew their horns, lit their torches, and smashed the empty jars. The Midianites, thinking they were surrounded by a huge army, panicked.

When the three hundred trumpets sounded, the Lord caused the men throughout the [Midianite] camp to turn on each other with their swords. The army fled.   *Judges 7:22*

GOD'S PROMISES TO THE DOUBTER

Gideon was used by God despite his many moments of doubt. The story reveals three promises God gives to the doubter.

EVIDENCE FOR THE SINCERE SEEKER

God was patient with Gideon's doubts. Four times God gave Gideon signs that he would lead the Israelites to victory. Some people picture God as someone who is hovering over us, ready to condemn us the first time we doubt His word. But one of God's characteristics is patience.

The Lord is not slow in keeping his promise, as some understand slowness. He is patient with you, not wanting anyone to perish, but everyone to come to repentance.   *2 Peter 3:9*

When you have honest doubts driven by difficult circumstances or a desire to know the truth, God is patient with you. A famous philosopher said, "There is more faith, believe me, in honest doubt, than in half our creeds." A sincere doubt, driven by a desire to seek out the truth, can produce a well-grounded faith. Chuck Colson heard the testimony of Tom Phillips, a Christian friend, and was deeply convicted. But he had some doubts which drove him to take the time to study the Scriptures for himself. God patiently revealed himself to Charles Colson. As a result of his personal study, Colson was born again and has become a powerful apologist for the Christian faith.

When God made man, He separated him from the animals by giving him the ability to reason. We have rational minds, intelligence, and a hunger for logic and order. Many people assume that putting your faith in God means checking your mind at the door and accepting God's Word against all "logic." That is not the case at all. God patiently revealed himself to Gideon, giving him solid evidence on four separate occasions. In the same way, God will give to the sincere seeker solid evidence to support His promises.

Faith will always be a necessary part of being a Christian, because we were not eyewitnesses of the creation of the world, the miracles of the Bible, the resurrection of Christ, or the writing of God's Word. But we are not asked to accept those truths by "blind faith."

Suppose I got onto a small airplane and a stranger was sitting in the cockpit. Suppose I asked the stranger, "Do you have your pilot's license?"

If he were to reply, "Just trust me," and I knew nothing about him, I would be flying by "blind faith." That would be stupid.

But if he were to say, "Yes, I was educated by Russ Summay" (a friend of mine who is a pilot instructor) and he were to show me his pilot's license, and if Russ Summay had told me the man was an excellent pilot, then I would not be flying by "blind faith." Although I would still be putting my faith in the pilot, it would be based on the evidences I had seen and heard. The apostles felt the same way about their faith. They believed because of the evidences they had seen. Peter wrote:

We did not follow cleverly invented stories when we told you about the power and coming of our Lord Jesus Christ, but we were <u>eyewitnesses</u> of his majesty.
2 Peter 1:16, emphasis added

God has given us evidence to reassure our faith. We have a well-designed universe that proves an intelligent being was involved. We can document the life, death, and resurrection of God's Son, Jesus. We have God's written Word, the Bible. And we can witness the dramatically changed lives of Christians throughout history. Jesus promised, "Seek and you will find" (Matthew 7:7). God will show evidence of His truth to the sincere seeker.

I have counseled many seekers to consider several great books by modern Christian writers on the topic of evidences for our faith: *Evidence That Demands a Verdict, More Evidence That Demands a Verdict,* and *More Than a Carpenter* by Josh McDowell; *Mere Christianity* by C. S. Lewis; and *In the Beginning* (a book describing scientific evidences for the belief in creation) by Dr. Walter Brown. Dr. Harold Morris and Dr. Duane Gish have also written extensively on scientific evidences for creation, and Ravi Zacharias, Charles Colson, and Francis Schaeffer have written several great books about the reasons for our faith. I am sure there are many others.

SALVATION FOR THE OBEDIENT BELIEVER

The Lord said to Gideon, "With the three hundred men that lapped [the water] I will save you and give the Midianites into your hands."   *Judges 7:7*

I have heard preachers manipulate audiences into making "decisions" for Christ by saying at the invitation time, "If you doubt your salvation at all. . . if you have any doubt you are going to Heaven, and you want to go to Heaven, I want you to come forward today and be saved." I feel uncomfortable with those types of invitations. It is true that the believer shouldn't doubt his salvation, but we all have doubts on occasion. I know I am saved by grace, but sometimes after I have sinned it's hard for me to comprehend that God could forgive me once again.

When we have those feelings of doubt, we don't need to be saved all over again. We just need reassurance that our lack of faith doesn't separate us from God. A father once brought his demon-possessed boy to Jesus and said,

"If you can do anything, take pity on us and help us."
"'If you can'?" said Jesus. "Everything is possible for him who believes."
Immediately the boy's father exclaimed, "I do believe; help me overcome my unbelief!"   *Mark 9:23, 24*

Is that not like all of us who believe? Yes, we believe. But we need help with our unbelief. I heard about a bridge that was built with a kite string. A construction worker flew a kite across the chasm to someone waiting on the other side. A rope was then attached to the kite string and pulled across the chasm. Then a cable was attached to the rope, then a series of cables, and so on. Eventually a sturdy bridge was built. You may sometimes feel like your faith is nothing more than a kite string. But

Jesus said if we had even the smallest amount of true faith, as small as a mustard seed, we could move mountains. No one has faith even that strong, yet God saves us anyway.

For it is by grace you have been saved, through faith—and this not from yourselves, it is the gift of God—not by works, so that no one can boast.   *Ephesians 2:8, 9*

VICTORY TO THE FAITHFUL

During that night the Lord said to Gideon, "Get up, go down against the camp, because I am going to give it into your hands."   *Judges 7:9*

God did what He said He would do, and Gideon won the victory. The story of Gideon is inspiring because we learn that victory does not depend upon our level of faith. Gideon obviously didn't have much faith, since it took four different miracles to convince him God was really in it. Yet Gideon finally took the one step of faith God required. Someone said faith is going to the edge of all the light you have, then taking one more step. Gideon obeyed, even though he doubted. He gathered the men and boldly went to face the enemy. He was surely afraid. He probably still wasn't the best example of faith, shaking in his sandals on the hillside. But he had taken the step God required, and God granted him victory because of it.

When you face battles in life—opposition from unbelievers, physical illness, a rebellious child, a lost relationship or some other challenge—you will be tempted to think God could not possibly grant victory to someone with so little faith. But He can, if you will act on the little faith you have and obey even when you doubt. Doubt is an emotion. Faith is a decision. When we decide to obey God, even when we doubt, God considers us faithful and grants us the victory.

So do not throw away your confidence; it will be richly rewarded. You need to persevere so that when you have done the will of God, you will receive what he has promised. For in just a very little while,

"He who is coming will come and will not delay.
But my righteous one will live by faith.
And if he shrinks back,
I will not be pleased with him."

But we are not of those who shrink back and are destroyed, but of those who believe and are saved.
Now faith is being sure of what we hope for and certain of what we do not see. . . . And without faith it is impossible to please God, because anyone who comes to him must believe that he exists and that he rewards those who earnestly seek him.   *Hebrews 10:35-39; 11:1, 6*

This is the victory that has overcome the world, even our faith.   *1 John 5:4*

IN TIMES OF LONELINESS

Ruth 1–4

When Gene Appel was twenty-nine years old, he was the successful minister of Central Christian Church in Las Vegas, Nevada. The church was growing, and they had just completed a new building. But on the night of the dedication service for their new church building, Gene's wife shocked him with the news that she was leaving him for a man she had met at work. He was heartbroken. All his efforts at reconciliation failed, and they were separated.

Gene immediately submitted his resignation to the church. But the elders studied, prayed, and counseled with both the minister and his wife, then concluded that Gene should stay as their minister. Though he had not been perfect, and perhaps had been too consumed with pastoring the church at times, he had been faithful to his wife and wanted to restore the relationship; she did not. Gene stayed at the church, and the people ministered to him through a difficult and lonely time in his life.

Gene says that the Christmas Eve after his separation he had the loneliest night of his life. "After our candlelight Christmas Eve service," he told me, "I intended to grab something to eat at a drive-thru, take it home, do some laundry, and pack for an early morning flight back to the midwest the next day to celebrate Christmas with my parents.

"I got away from church about 9:30 and I was starving. All I had to eat that day was a sandwich in the early afternoon. I started driving around on this cold and windy Christmas Eve and absolutely nothing was open. Taco Bell was closed. McDonald's was closed. Even the twenty-four-hour Food Mart was closed. I had never seen Las Vegas so quiet. Nobody was on the streets. It was like a ghost town.

"As I drove I began to picture everybody in their homes celebrating Christmas Eve, except me. Now I was starting to get depressed. I started to remember how as a boy our family always got together on Christmas Eve. But there was absolutely nothing to eat at my house and I was determined to find something.

"I went to Sam's Town, which is a country-and-western casino with some restaurants. To my surprise, the place was pretty busy. I walked up to their fifties-style diner and sat down alone at a table for four to order dinner. It was like a bad dream.

"I sat there eating the blue-plate special thinking, *I can't believe it. I just spoke for twenty-two hundred people and here I am at Sam's Town on Christmas Eve eating meat loaf and mashed potatoes alone.*

"Just when I thought it couldn't get any worse, someone put a quarter in the jukebox and Elvis began singing in my ear, 'Are you lonesome tonight?' Honestly, I just started laughing to myself—maybe to keep from crying. For a few moments that night I had some of the loneliest feelings of my life.

"The thought that overwhelmed me was *Gene, here you are, one of the most blessed guys in the world. You have a church that loves you, more friends than anyone should be legally allowed to have, and you're flying home in the morning to be with twenty members of your family for Christmas. If you, of all people, can experience these feelings of loneliness, imagine how life is for people who really have a reason to be lonely.*

"I gained a new empathy that night for lonely people. As I walked through the casino on my way out, I looked at all the people playing slot machines and table games on Christmas Eve and I thought, *They don't have anywhere to go either. They don't have anyone to be with tonight.* And it just broke my heart."

If you have felt lonely at times, you are not the only one. Statistics show that 15 percent of people in America feel lonely most or all of the time, and 78 percent feel lonely at least some of the time. Since one fifth of all households in America consist of a person living alone (a 385 percent increase over thirty years ago), it is not surprising that so many people battle loneliness.

People long for comfort in times of loneliness. No one has the ability to comfort us more than God himself. For a great illustration of God's promises in times of loneliness, let's consider the Old Testament story of Ruth.

RUTH'S REASONS FOR LONELINESS

Though people feel lonely for a variety of reasons, Ruth could sympathize with at least three of the most popular.

GRIEF

The book of Ruth opens with a few verses of background about Ruth and her mother-in-law, Naomi. Ruth, a Moabite woman, had married one of Naomi's sons, a Jewish man. They all had moved to Moab to escape a famine. But in ten years' time, Naomi's husband and two sons died, leaving Naomi, Ruth and Orpah, Ruth's sister-in-law, alone in Moab.

Losing a mate is one of the most difficult adjustments in life. The Bible says that in marriage the two become one. A person feels incomplete as well as grief stricken when he or she loses a spouse. It takes most people two years to become emotionally stable again after the death of a mate. Two lonely years can seem like an eternity during grief. One can wonder at times if life will ever be fulfilling and happy again.

One widow in our church told me that months after her husband's death, when something significant would happen during the day she would say to herself, "I have to tell Gerald about that tonight when he gets home." Then she would remember he had died five months ago, and she would think, "He will not be coming home tonight or ever." She would well up with tears again.

A more popular sense of grief today comes from the pain of divorce. A friend of mine who went through a bitter divorce told me that the experience was even worse than if his mate had died. I believe he is right. The pain of divorce is often worse than having to experience the death of a spouse, for several reasons:

- When someone dies you seldom blame yourself, but with divorce there are constant feelings of guilt.
- With death you say good-bye and know it is over, but in divorce you often keep seeing the person and reliving the feelings.
- When a mate dies you're left with positive feelings of love, but in a divorce you live with the reality of rejection.
- With the death of a spouse you will find the comfort of friends, but in divorce some of your friends will be lost altogether and the rest do not know what to say.

FAILURE

Ruth was not only grieving the loss of her husband, she was also childless, which in her culture would have made her feel like a failure. A sense of failure can cause feelings of loneliness. You are tempted to believe that you've let people down, that you're worthless, or that no one would want to befriend someone who has failed.

Being childless even in today's culture can often bring on the same feelings of failure and loneliness that Ruth experienced. While we may not put as much pressure on women to have children, most still feel a desire to do so. When they cannot, they are tempted to feel they have failed. Childless couples especially face such emotions in their later years. When their friends are celebrating Mother's Day, having grandchildren or enjoying a Thanksgiving meal with a large family, they may begin to fight feelings of loneliness and failure.

ISOLATION

Ruth's mother-in-law, Naomi, decided to return to her homeland. She said good-bye to her daughters-in-law and started home. But Ruth longed to be loyal to Naomi and to Naomi's God.

"Look," said Naomi, "your sister-in-law is going back to her people and her gods. Go back with her."

But Ruth replied, "Don't urge me to leave you or to turn back from you. Where you go I will go, and where you stay I will stay. Your people will be my people and your God my God. Where you die I will die, and there I will be buried. May the Lord deal with me, be it ever so severely, if anything but death separates you and me." Ruth 1:15-17

Ruth knew that Naomi followed the one true God, and she needed to follow Him, too. She was willing to leave her homeland to stay with the one she knew would lead her to Jehovah God. But in her new home in Judah, she must have felt isolated. She was in a foreign country with different customs, different languages, different foods. She certainly felt alone at times.

You would think people would most often feel lonely when they are truly alone. But you can feel isolated even when you're surrounded by people. The most lonely experience I ever had was my first year in college. I had never been away from home for more than a week. Now I was four hundred miles from home with no prospect of returning for two months. I found out what homesickness was all about. There were plenty of people there. The whole dorm was full of young men my age, and I even had two good roommates in my dorm room. But there was nobody who knew me. No one really cared about me. That first week, when I would go to bed at night, I would stare into the darkness, unable to sleep. I felt terribly alone. For several weeks I would tune the radio to KDKA in Pittsburgh and listen to the broadcast of the Pittsburgh Pirates baseball games, just to feel like I was connected to life at home, where we had always listened to those games on the radio.

People who are famous also experience loneliness in the midst of a crowd. We assume that successful people could not possibly be alone. They are strong, admired by others, and constantly encouraged. But there is a sense of isolation that often accompanies those who reach the top of their field. The higher one climbs in his career, the fewer peers he has and the fewer sympathizers. He usually has fewer friends. He might be respected and admired, but he is treated differently. He is tempted to treat others suspiciously, always aware that someone would like to knock him off the top rung of the ladder. I read an article once entitled, "The Lonely Whine of the Top Dog."

Following a successful concert, a popular singer wrote

in her diary, "Tonight I made love to twenty-five thousand people and went home alone."

H. G. Wells, who was once at the top of his field as a film director and author, said, "I am sixty-five years old and I am lonely. I have never known peace."

Albert Einstein said, "It is strange to be known so universally and yet be so lonely."

GOD'S PROMISES TO THE LONELY

Mother Teresa said, "Loneliness and the feeling of being uncared-for and unwanted are the greatest poverty." But God has promised to help us through our times of loneliness. We never have to feel uncared for or unwanted. God has promised His comfort, His blessing, and His guidance whenever we feel alone.

GOD WILL COMFORT YOU IF YOU TRUST IN HIM
Many are the woes of the wicked,
but the Lord's unfailing love
surrounds the man who trusts in him.   *Psalm 32:10*

Ruth made the right decision to follow Jehovah God. Her Moabite gods could not have brought her comfort in times of loneliness and grief. But we serve a God who is always present, and who loves us unconditionally. Though Christians feel lonely at times, we should remember the promises of our loving heavenly Father. We are never alone.

Be strong and courageous. Do not be afraid or terrified . . . for the Lord your God goes with you; he will never leave you nor forsake you.   *Deuteronomy 31:6*

GOD WILL BLESS YOU IF YOU WORK HARD
There is an old saying, "Idle hands are the devil's workshop." Ruth decided she would not sit around waiting for

something to happen to her in Judah. To do so would have only enhanced her feelings of loneliness. Ruth went to work picking up the leftover grain in the fields. The welfare system of that day required that the reapers not harvest a field a second time, but leave the leftovers for the poor. Ruth went through the fields behind the harvesters and worked hard to put some bread on the table.

The sluggard craves and gets nothing,
but the desires of the diligent are fully satisfied.

Proverbs 13:4

Whatever your hand finds to do, do it with all your might.

Ecclesiastes 9:10

Hard work cures loneliness by filling our time, giving us a sense of self-worth and helping us gain the respect of others. More importantly, there is no better cure for loneliness or depression than doing something good for somebody else.

He who has been stealing must steal no longer, but must work, doing something useful with his own hands, that he may have something to share with those in need.

Ephesians 4:28

Ruth could have moped around her new home in Judah, allowing others to feel sorry for her, demanding that others take care of her, and praying that God would hurry up and give her a new husband. Instead Ruth desired to work hard, not only for herself, but for her mother-in-law. And God rewarded her diligence.

GOD WILL GUIDE YOU IF YOU ARE PATIENT

You have probably witnessed someone make a terrible mistake because he or she was not patient during a time of loneliness. A single person might compromise her convictions for a one-night stand rather than wait till she finds someone who will stay faithful to her for life; then she regrets it later. Another might marry too quickly after a divorce, only to wake up several months later with someone he really doesn't know. Other lonely people might turn to alcohol or drugs, or to a false religion, rather than depending on the Lord and patiently waiting for Him to cure their loneliness in His time.

I have seen well-meaning singles chase away potential mates because they are too anxious. Ruth didn't make that mistake. She found herself gleaning in the fields of a relative of her late husband, a man named Boaz. The custom by law in those days stated that the closest relative of a man who died was responsible for caring for—even marrying, if possible—the man's widow. It would have been tempting for Ruth to run up to her rich relative Boaz, demand that he become her "kinsman-redeemer," and propose to him on the spot! But such action would certainly have been a turn-off to Boaz, so she waited.

Ruth impressed Boaz with her integrity. He noted later that she didn't run after the younger men, neither the rich nor the poor, and she had established herself in town as a woman of noble character. Boaz treated Ruth kindly, making sure that his workers left a little extra for her in the fields, and even inviting her to eat dinner with him. Her heart must have raced as she sat across the dinner table from this wealthy man, wondering if God were providing a cure for her loneliness! But Ruth didn't lose patience. She continued to work hard, maintain her integrity, and care for her mother-in-law, Naomi. She waited for the Lord's timing.

Then the time came. Naomi told Ruth it was the right time for her to propose to Boaz. That's right, she proposed to him! Evidently Boaz was an older man, and perhaps out of kindness had left Ruth alone. Naomi instructed Ruth to put on her best clothes and perfume, then go down to the threshing floor and lie down at Boaz's feet after he had gone to sleep. This wasn't an immoral provocation, but a common form of proposal in that day. Ruth prepared herself as a bride and made it known to Boaz that she was available.

In the middle of the night, something startled [Boaz], and he turned and discovered a woman lying at his feet.

"Who are you?" he asked.

"I am your servant Ruth," she said. "Spread the corner of your garment over me, since you are a kinsman-redeemer."

"The Lord bless you, my daughter," he replied. "This kindness is greater than that which you showed earlier: You have not run after the younger men, whether rich or poor."

Ruth 3:8-10

God rewarded her patience, and Boaz agreed to become her kinsman-redeemer. Ruth's loneliness had come to an end. They were married.

God also rewarded Ruth in another way. Ruth and Boaz had a son. Their son, Obed, later became the grandfather of King David, and the ancestor of Jesus the Messiah. Ruth the Moabitess had become a part of the ancestral line of the Messiah, because of her patience and faithfulness during a time of loneliness.

God will do the same for you. He will comfort you in your loneliness, reward your obedience, and guide you through your lonely time if you are patient.

Jim Irby, a minister in Cincinnati, Ohio, often tells of visiting an old Indian squaw who lived alone in a rugged log cabin in the Kiamichi mountains of Oklahoma. She was sitting in her rocker on the front porch when he drove up. He got out of the car and called, "Are you all alone, ma'am?"

"Well, son," she responded, "It's just me and Jesus!"

If the Lord is our companion, we need never feel lonely, even when we are alone.

[Jesus said], "And surely I am with you always, to the very end of the age."   *Matthew 28:20*

Trust in the Lord with all your heart
   and lean not on your own understanding;
in all your ways acknowledge him,
    and he will make your paths straight.   *Proverbs 3:5-6*

I waited patiently for the Lord;
   he turned to me and heard my cry. . . .
He put a new song in my mouth,
   a hymn of praise to our God.
Many will see and fear
   and put their trust in the Lord.   *Psalm 40:1, 3*

Who shall separate us from the love of Christ? Shall trouble or hardship or persecution or famine or nakedness or danger or sword? . . . For I am convinced that neither death nor life, neither angels nor demons, neither the present nor the future, nor any powers, neither height nor depth, nor anything else in all creation, will be able to separate us from the love of God that is in Christ Jesus our Lord.
      Romans 8:35, 38, 39

IN TIMES OF FINANCIAL STRESS

1 Kings 17:1–6

It probably wouldn't surprise you to learn that most Americans have trouble with money.

- Four out of five Americans owe more than they own.
- Forty percent borrow more than they can make monthly payments on.
- The average American family is three weeks away from bankruptcy.
- According to Social Security, eight-five out of one hundred Americans have less than $250 in cash saved by age sixty-five.
- The average American gives less than 2 percent to charitable institutions. The average church member gives 2.5 percent.
- Approximately 50 percent of all divorces are caused by or related to financial pressures in the home. The most secretive and sensitive subject in most marriages is not sexuality, but finances.

No wonder Jesus had so much to say about money! Sixteen of His thirty-eight parables were about money matters. Jesus spoke more often about stewardship than

He did about Heaven or Hell. He talked about money five times more often than He talked about prayer.

The words of Christ and the promises of God throughout the New and Old Testaments regarding money are both comforting and challenging. But let's first note what God does not promise us in times of financial stress.

GOD DOES NOT PROMISE MATERIAL WEALTH

In any discussion about the blessings of God during financial hardships, there is a danger that people will fall into the false theology some call the "health and wealth" gospel. Tammy Faye Bakker used to say, "If you pray for a new car, make sure to tell God what color you want, because you are going to get it!" God is not some kind of genie waiting for you to make a wish.

The Bible *does* say that the righteous man has a better chance of prosperity, since he is honest, a hard worker, and does not spend his money wastefully. The proverbs promise:

The wages of the righteous bring them life,
but the income of the wicked brings them
punishment.   *Proverbs 10:16*

The blessing of the Lord brings wealth,
and he adds no trouble to it.   *Proverbs 10:22*

No harm befalls the righteous,
but the wicked have their fill of trouble.
                        Proverbs 12:21

Diligent hands will rule,
but laziness ends in slave labor.   *Proverbs 12:24*

But the Bible also talks about the *wicked* occasionally getting rich because of their evil deeds and their oppression of the poor, so riches are certainly not an indication of spirituality. The Scriptures indicate that "it rains on the

just and the unjust." Good things and bad things happen
to good and bad people, irrespective of their belief in
God. The Dallas Cowboys won the Super Bowl and
cashed in on huge bonus checks, even though some of
the Cowboys have notorious reputations for wild living.

Many righteous people in the Bible were wealthy, but
there were many who were poor as well. Jesus said of
himself, "Foxes have holes and birds of the air have nests,
but the Son of Man has no place to lay his head"
(Matthew 8:20).

There were also men like Paul who knew both poverty
and wealth as a result of following God's commands.
Paul wrote,

*"I have learned to be content whatever the circumstances. I
know what it is to be in need, and I know what it is to have
plenty. I have learned the secret of being content in any and
every situation, whether well fed or hungry, whether living in
plenty or in want. I can do everything through him who gives
me strength."*   *Philippians 4:11-13*

GOD DOES NOT PROMISE FINANCIAL SECURITY
*[Jesus said],"In this world you will have trouble. But take
heart! I have overcome the world.*   *"John 16:33*

God doesn't promise us freedom from financial hardships. In fact, James wrote, "Consider it pure joy, my
brothers, whenever you face trials of many kinds." (James
1:2, emphasis added). He did not say if you face trials,
but whenever. Trials in this world are inevitable.

In 1 Kings 17, Elijah the Tishbite was called upon to be
the mouth of God during the reign of Ahab, one of the
most wicked rulers in the history of Israel. Elijah went to
Ahab and said, "As the Lord, the God of Israel, lives,
whom I serve, there will be neither dew nor rain in the
next few years except at my word" (1 Kings 17:1).

You would think that God would reward Elijah for his boldness before the king. Surely Elijah wouldn't be made to suffer from the famine. Surely he was allowed to go to a foreign country and feast like a king because of his obedience. But that's not what happened to Elijah.

Then the word of the Lord came to Elijah: "Leave here, turn eastward and hide in the Kerith Ravine, east of the Jordan. You will drink from the brook, and I have ordered the ravens to feed you there."　　　　　*1 Kings 17:2-4*

For his faithfulness, Elijah was called to hide out in a ravine, drink the water there (until it later dried up), and be fed by ravens! Those were not exactly enviable accommodations! As the brook began to dry up, the water probably became warm, stagnant, and full of algae. Ravens were not the ideal waiters, either. The Scripture says that ravens brought him bread and meat in the morning and bread and meat in the evening. That may not sound too bad unless you know something about ravens. The Israelites weren't allowed to eat ravens "because they are detestable" (see Leviticus 11:13-15). Ravens are scavengers who will eat just about anything. They like to store their food in cow dung to keep it from freezing. Elijah probably couldn't help wondering where those ravens had been just before they got their delivery orders from God!

PROMISES IN FINANCIAL STRESS

While God does not promise you wealth, or even freedom from financial hardships, He does promise to take care of you through those hardships. Here are three promises you can depend on during financial stress.

BASIC PROVISIONS FOR THE BELIEVER
[Jesus said], "Look at the birds of the air; they do not sow or

*reap or store away in barns, and yet your heavenly Father
feeds them. Are you not much more valuable than they? . . .*

*"See how the lilies of the field grow. They do not labor or
spin. Yet I tell you that not even Solomon in all his splendor
was dressed like one of these. If that is how God clothes the
grass of the field, which is here today and tomorrow is thrown
into the fire, will he not much more clothe you, O you of little faith?"* Matthew 6:26, 28-30

If God makes sure that the birds have enough to eat,
and if God went to the trouble of sending ravens to provide for Elijah even in the Kerith Ravine, He will make
sure you are fed and clothed. God does not promise
riches, but He does promise to care for your basic needs.
Paul wrote, "And my God will meet all your needs according to his glorious riches in Christ Jesus" (Philippians 4:19).

Consider the words of the psalmist:

The Lord is my shepherd, I shall not be in want.
Psalm 23:1

*The lions may grow weak and hungry,
   but those who seek the Lord lack no good thing.*
Psalm 34:10

*I was young and now I am old,
   yet I have never seen the righteous forsaken
   or their children begging bread.*
Psalm 37:25

FREEDOM FROM WORRY

When we understand God's promise to take care of
our needs, we gain another blessing: freedom from
worry. We will discuss God's promises in times of worry
in more detail later. But it is worth noting here, in a
chapter on financial stress, that God does not want us to
worry.

America is the richest nation in the history of the world, yet as a nation we are hooked on drugs that are meant to curb our anxieties. Tranquilizers, alcohol, and sleeping pills are regularly consumed to ease the pain of worry. Jesus commanded:

"So do not worry, saying, 'What shall we eat?' or 'What shall we drink?' or 'What shall we wear?' For the pagans run after all these things, and your heavenly Father knows that you need them. But seek first his kingdom and his righteousness, and all these things will be given to you as well."

Matthew 6:31-33

Worry is not just a problem for the poverty stricken. In fact, the more riches someone has, the more he has to worry about. My friend Ron Decker told me about getting a new sports car. In his youth he had dreamed of owning a Corvette, but he became a schoolteacher so his chances were slim. However, he was single for a long time, so he had the chance to save up, and finally bought a beautiful metallic blue Corvette.

He said for the first couple of weeks he loved it. But then he grew tired of hearing remarks like, "We must be paying schoolteachers too much these days." He worried about getting it scratched, so he would take up two spaces in the parking lot. When he returned, he'd find nasty notes on the windshield. He started parking in the back of the lot and walking the extra distance. He discovered that police were more likely to stop a Corvette because he was automatically suspected of speeding. He worried about someone stealing the car, so he had a theft alarm put in it. Then it would go off in the middle of the night and wake up half the people in his apartment complex. He said after a few months, he was glad to get rid of it.

The wise man prayed:

Give me neither poverty nor riches,
   but give me only my daily bread.
Otherwise, I may have too much and disown you
   and say, 'Who is the Lord?'
Or I may become poor and steal,
   and so dishonor the name of my God.   Proverbs 30:8, 9

It may be more difficult for the rich man to trust in God and not worry about his material things, but God can free even the rich man from the bonds of worry. The Bible does not condemn wealthy people. However, Scriptures do warn against the dangers of *wanting* to be rich. The secret to trusting in God and being free from your worries is twofold: learning to be content with whatever God has given you, and being generous with what He has entrusted to you.

But godliness with contentment is great gain. For we brought nothing into the world, and we can take nothing out of it. But if we have food and clothing, we will be content with that. People who want to get rich fall into temptation and a trap and into many foolish and harmful desires that plunge men into ruin and destruction. For the love of money is a root of all kinds of evil. Some people, eager for money, have wandered from the faith and pierced themselves with many griefs. . . .

Command those who are rich in this present world not to be arrogant nor to put their hope in wealth, which is so uncertain, but to put their hope in God, who richly provides us with everything for our enjoyment. Command them to do good, to be rich in good deeds, and to be generous and willing to share. In this way they will lay up treasure for themselves as a firm foundation for the coming age, so that they may take hold of the life that is truly life.   1 Timothy 6:6-10, 17-19

BLESSINGS FOR THE GENEROUS

God promises blessings, both material and spiritual, for those who are generous with their possessions.

God promises material blessings for the tither. While God does not promise freedom from all financial hardships, nor does He promise wealth for every believer, He does make an extraordinary promise in the book of Malachi:

"Bring the whole tithe into the storehouse, that there may be food in my house. Test me in this," says the Lord Almighty, "and see if I will not throw open the floodgates of heaven and pour out so much blessing that you will not have room enough for it. I will prevent pests from devouring your crops, and the vines in your fields will not cast their fruit," says the Lord Almighty. Malachi 3:10-12

You can't out-give God. I have witnessed that to be true in my own life. To my knowledge, this is the only passage in the Bible where the Lord challenges the believer to "test" Him. Test God and see if His promise is true. You give one-tenth of your income, and He will "throw open the floodgates of heaven and pour out so much blessing that you will not have room enough for it." I believe God will make the 90 percent remaining seem like 110 percent. Your refrigerator will run a little bit longer, or your car will not break down as easily, or you will find financial gain where you thought there was none. It is difficult to explain, but I believe it is a true spiritual principle: the Lord will bless you financially if you tithe. You may not get "rich" by the world's standards, and you may not have everything you want, but you will feel blessed with plenty of material provisions and a spirit of contentment. Test Him.

God promises spiritual blessings for the sacrificial giver. What if I were to show you an investment fund that had a 10,000 percent return on it at retirement? For every dollar you put in today, you will receive one hundred dollars at retirement—whether you are twenty years old or fifty years old today. If you invest ten thousand dollars now, you will receive one million dollars on the day you retire. Jesus Christ promised just that—a 10,000 percent return on your investment the day you "retire" from the Christian life (that is, the day of your death).

[Jesus said], "And everyone who has left houses or brothers or sisters or father or mother or children or fields for my sake will receive a hundred times as much and will inherit eternal life."   *Matthew 19:29*

Great eternal rewards await the person who is willing to give generously for Christ's sake in this life. Jesus promised that God will give to us using the same measure of generosity we have used in giving to others:

"Give, and it will be given to you. A good measure, pressed down, shaken together and running over, will be poured into your lap. For with the measure you use, it will be measured to you."   *Luke 6:38*

There's a great old parable about a beggar who asked a king for a gift. The king said, "First, what do you have to give to me?" The beggar had one small sack of corn hidden in his cloak. He was afraid the king would take advantage of him, so he reached into his cloak and pulled out the smallest kernel of corn he could find, hoping the king would think that was all he had. He handed it to the king. The king then reached into his bag of gold and handed the beggar a piece of gold the same size as his kernel of corn. How the man wished he had given the king all he had!

The practice of tithing was introduced in the Old Testament and was not repeated in the New Testament.

Christians are not bound by the tithe law. Instead, we are simply commanded to give generously.

But how do you determine what is generous? When you eat at a restaurant, how do you tip a good waiter? The standard is 15 percent. If you want to be generous, how much do you give? You would give more than 15 percent.

God is not our waiter, but our Lord. He owns it all, and we are just stewards of what He has given us. In the Old Testament He commanded that we return 10 percent to Him. In the New Testament, after He gives us His Son Jesus, the promise of eternal life, the Holy Spirit, the Bible, and the church, He simply asks that we give generously. What would you consider generous giving?

Remember this: Whoever sows sparingly will also reap sparingly, and whoever sows generously will also reap generously. Each man should give what he has decided in his heart to give, not reluctantly or under compulsion, for God loves a cheerful giver. And God is able to make all grace abound to you, so that in all things at all times, having all that you need, you will abound in every good work.

2 Corinthians 9:6-8

Our family used to play board games together on vacation trips. On one particular night when we were playing Monopoly, I was really on a roll. The first time around the board I landed on Boardwalk. The next time around I landed on Park Place! Before long I owned all four railroads and Indiana, Illinois, and Kentucky Avenues. I knew I was unstoppable. Within an hour I had hotels on every property and I was raking it in. Someone would land on my property and I would smirk, "That's five hundred dollars! Oh, wait, I have a hotel on that one! That's one thousand dollars!" One by one, the other family members went bankrupt.

Finally, the last person went bankrupt and I was the Monopoly champ. The rest of the family trudged off to bed. I said, "Wait a minute! Someone has to clean this up!"

"That's the prize for winning, Dad!" they retorted. "You get to clean up the game."

Suddenly there I sat. I was surrounded by wealth, and no friends! The game was over. I picked up the pieces, placed them back in the box, put the money back, and closed the lid.

That night as I lay in bed, I remembered hearing Dr. James Dobson compare the Christian life to a Monopoly game. How empty we will feel if we stand before God someday and our emphasis throughout our lifetime has been on material things. Suddenly all the wealth we've accumulated won't matter. We have to leave it behind. What will matter will be whether or not we were honest, compassionate, and generous with what God has given us.

[Jesus said], "Do not store up for yourselves treasures on earth, where moth and rust destroy, and where thieves break in and steal. But store up for yourselves treasures in heaven, where moth and rust do not destroy, and where thieves do not break in and steal. For where your treasure is, there your heart will be also." Matthew 6:19-21

Author Bob Benson compared this life to a picnic. He would challenge you to picture yourself alone at a picnic with your bologna sandwich. Suddenly a family that you recognize approaches, sits near you and begins to break out their picnic lunch. They have fried chicken, potato salad, coleslaw, baked beans, cherry pie, and all the fixin's. Then they say to you, "Bob, it's kind of our practice that we share everything we have. Why don't you join us. If you will pitch in and share your bologna sandwich, we'll share our lunch with you." Would you share that bologna sandwich? Who wouldn't?

God owns all things, and He asks us to be stewards of just a little bit on this earth. Then He says, "Why don't we just put it all together? You share what you have been given, and I'll share what I have." Wouldn't it be foolish to be stingy with what God has given us?

When you are facing financial pressures, remember: God promises us daily provisions, an eternal perspective, a spirit of contentment, freedom from worry, and treasures in heaven, if we will trust in Him, and be generous with what we have been given.

IN TIMES
OF TEMPTATION

Numbers 22:1–40

A little boy had saved all winter long to buy a new baseball glove. Early in the summer he needed just one dollar more to have enough money for the glove he wanted. One night he prayed, "Dear God, help me to earn the rest of the money for a baseball glove, and please don't let the ice cream truck come down my street!"

Nobody likes to battle temptation. We wish we could either avoid it altogether, or go ahead and give in to the temptation when it gets too tough. Oscar Wilde said, "I can resist anything but temptation."

But just like financial trials, God does not promise to exempt us from times of temptation. He does, however, promise to help us through those times. Before we examine those promises, let's study one man in the Old Testament who battled temptation much the same way we do. There's a strange and humorous story in Numbers 22 about a pagan sorcerer named Balaam. He is used by God to speak to his king, Balak, the king of Moab. Balaam faced temptations to do his own will instead of God's will. The temptations he faced and the ways he handled them are reminiscent of the battles many of us wage against temptation every day.

BALAAM'S BATTLES

The Israelites were preparing to attack their enemy, the Moabites. The king of Moab, Balak, was afraid because he knew the Israelites were powerful and of great number. Balak heard that an internationally known fortune-teller, a soothsayer named Balaam, was not too far away, so he sent a group of messengers to get Balaam.

The elders of Moab and Midian left, taking with them the fee for divination. When they came to Balaam, they told him what Balak had said. Numbers 22:7

THE TEMPTATION OF NOTORIETY

Wow! The king of Moab is calling for me! Balaam must have thought. Most of us are tempted by the opportunity to impress other people. If we have the chance to impress the governor, the owner of a large corporation, the principal of our school, the star quarterback or the prom queen, it can be a great temptation to us. While "being famous" isn't a sin in itself (Jesus was the most famous person of all time), the desire for fame and notoriety is not godly. It can drive us to do stupid and immoral things if we don't resist it.

The king was asking Balaam to curse the Israelites. Balaam was most familiar with evil spirits, who would speak to him as if they were gods and would imitate the truth. This time he got the real thing.

God came to Balaam and asked, "Who are these men with you?"

Balaam said to God, "Balak son of Zippor, king of Moab, sent me this message." Numbers 22:9, 10

"Wait till you hear this one, God! Balak, the king of Moab, has come asking me for advice! I'm famous!"

Theodore Roosevelt's daughter said her dad wanted to

be the bride at every wedding and the corpse at every funeral. J. Wallace Hamilton called it the *drum major instinct*. We want to be important, to achieve distinction, to lead the parade. We are tempted to think, If I could just be the best at something—*just one thing where I was better than everybody else—then I would feel fulfilled.*

If someone were to say that you could make it big in the movies, or be the star of the team, or be a model, that would have tremendous appeal. It can create a great temptation to chase after fame instead of the will of God. Carl Sandburg said, "We all want to play Hamlet."

Balaam was given the chance to be famous, to stand before the king and proclaim "God's message." It would be a tremendous temptation to bend the truth a little and say whatever the king wanted to hear.

But God said to Balaam, "Do not go with them. You must not put a curse on those people, because they are blessed."
The next morning Balaam got up and said to Balak's princes, "Go back to your own country, for the Lord has refused to let me go with you." Numbers 22:12, 13

This time Balaam resisted the temptation for fame and didn't go. But King Balak wouldn't take no for an answer. Balaam would face two additional temptations.

Then Balak sent other princes, more numerous and more distinguished than the first. They came to Balaam and said:
"This is what Balak son of Zippor says: Do not let anything keep you from coming to me, because I will reward you handsomely and do whatever you say. Come and put a curse on these people for me." Numbers 22:15-17

THE TEMPTATION OF PEER PRESSURE
The temptation to be famous is strong, but the temptation to be accepted by your peers is even stronger. Most

of us would like to be famous, but we don't mind too much if we are not. Balaam was able to resist that temptation with some ease. But most of us have an intense desire to please our peers. Nobody likes to let other people down, or to stand out in a crowd for the wrong reasons, with the crowd against you.

Simon Peter had vowed he would die for Christ, but all it took was a little peer pressure to break him. Why do young people begin smoking or drinking? Why do people use profanity when they are telling a joke? Why do we pay enormous amounts of money to buy a nice-looking automobile? Almost always, we do those things because we want to fit in with our peers.

I once got off the elevator and realized I was on the wrong floor. The doors hadn't closed, but I was too proud to get back on the elevator and admit I was wrong. I headed down the hall and went up the steps! I had a tremendous desire to impress a bunch of strangers who I will probably never see again!

THE TEMPTATION OF WEALTH

With the temptation of peer pressure came a third temptation. The king's men promised to reward Balaam "handsomely."

A philosopher once asked a female acquaintance if she would go to bed with him for one million dollars. She said, "Of course."

"Would you do it for one hundred dollars?" he asked.

"What kind of woman do you take me for?" she responded.

"We've already established that," he said. "Now we're just haggling over the price."

I hear people say that everyone has a price. Really? If so, that is a shame. Is the temptation for wealth so strong in all of us that there is not one who would maintain his convictions no matter what the price?

Many do give in. The desire for wealth is a strong temptation. People say, "I can cheat on my income taxes and no one will know; I can pad my expense account because everyone does it; I can get the sale if I keep quiet about the defect; I can give more later if I invest my tithe in this stock now; I can make money off this restaurant, but only if I sell alcohol."

At first Balaam appeared to stand firm against these latter two temptations. He told the princes:

"Even if Balak gave me his palace filled with silver and gold, I could not do anything great or small to go beyond the command of the Lord my God."   Numbers 22:18

But then Balaam added:

"Now stay here tonight as the others did, and I will find out what else the Lord will tell me."   Numbers 22:19

The Bible warns against giving the devil a "foothold" (Ephesians 4:27). Balaam had done just that. He knew what God wanted him to say, but he was flirting with temptation. "Riches are no temptation to me," Balaam boasted. "But stay the night, and let me try God again. Maybe He'll change His mind."

An overweight preacher announced to his staff that he was going on a diet, then appeared the next day with a dozen chocolate donuts. His secretary said, "I thought you were on a diet."

"I was, but God wants me off of it," the preacher explained. "I drove by the bakery and I prayed, 'Lord, if You don't want me to buy any donuts, don't allow there to be an open parking place in front of the bakery.' Wouldn't you know it! The eighth time I drove around the block there was a space right by the door! I figured it must be God's will."

God will not take away our free will. If we continue to flirt with temptation, He won't force us to stay away. God said to Balaam, "Fine, go with the men" (22:20, my paraphrase). But God was not happy with Balaam.

But God was very angry when he went, and the angel of the Lord stood in the road to oppose him. Balaam was riding on his donkey, and his two servants were with him. When the donkey saw the angel of the Lord standing in the road with a drawn sword in his hand, she turned off the road into a field. Balaam beat her to get her back on the road.

Numbers 22:22, 23

Balaam's donkey was more spiritually sensitive than Balaam was! She could see there was an angel in her way—angry and with his sword drawn! After Balaam beat the animal three times, God did a miraculous and humorous thing to get Balaam's attention:

Then the Lord opened the donkey's mouth, and she said to Balaam, "What have I done to you to make you beat me these three times?"

Numbers 22:28

I would've been stunned! But Balaam was used to sorcery, demonic tricks, and strange sights. I don't think he realized that his donkey talking was unusual. He started arguing with his donkey!

Balaam answered the donkey, "You have made a fool of me! If I had a sword in my hand, I would kill you right now."

Numbers 22:29

The donkey said, "Look, Balaam, I've been your donkey a long time. Do I usually act this way?" Balaam admitted that the donkey didn't usually behave in such an obstinate manner, but he was irritated with her for not doing what he wanted her to do. Finally, the Lord opened Balaam's eyes so he could see the angel standing before them. Balaam immediately repented before the angel. He admitted he had been disobedient, and he asked the angel if he should go back home.

The angel of the Lord said to Balaam, "Go with the men, but speak only what I tell you." So Balaam went with the princes of Balak.　　　　　　　　　　*Numbers 22:35*

Balaam had given in to the temptations of fame, peer pressure, and wealth. But God forgave him anyway. Because Balaam turned and obeyed God, and spoke only the words God gave him, the Lord used him to speak mighty and powerful words to King Balak. Balaam refused to curse God's chosen people, so he was not very popular with the king. But he was obedient to God, at least for a time, and his prophetic words are forever recorded for us in the Old Testament.

PROMISES TO THE TEMPTED

Much like Balaam, we find ourselves yielding to the desires for fame, popularity, acceptance among our peers, wealth, pleasure, and power. If we do yield, we feel so foolish later, and we end up asking, "Why did I do such a stupid thing?"

Satan knows human nature. One wise preacher said, "The devil knows the precise bait each of us prefers. He's been fishing for souls longer than anyone else on earth. He knows our weaknesses in appetite and spends time trying to get us to strike at his bait." But in times of temptation, God gives us two specific promises to help us resist Satan's bait.

TEMPTATION IS INEVITABLE

When tempted, no one should say, "God is tempting me." For God cannot be tempted by evil, nor does he tempt anyone;

but each one is tempted when, by his own evil desire, he is
dragged away and enticed.   *James 1:13, 14*

A pseudopious Christian boasted, "I never encounter
the devil!"

But a wise saint responded, "That's understandable.
Two people going down the same path in the same direction seldom bump into one another."

God doesn't promise to exempt us from temptations.
Even Jesus was tempted. We know Satan tested him three
times in the wilderness after Jesus' baptism. Then Luke
4:13 says, "When the devil had finished all this tempting,
he left him until an opportune time." Jesus faced contin-
ual temptations—and from the master of deception, Satan
himself!

Because he himself suffered when he was tempted, he is able
to help those who are being tempted. . . .
For we do not have a high priest who is unable to sympathize
with our weaknesses, but we have one [Jesus] who has been
tempted in every way, just as we are—yet was without sin. Let
us then approach the throne of grace with confidence, so that
we may receive mercy and find grace to help us in our time
of need.   *Hebrews 2:18; 4:15, 16*

TEMPTATION CAN BE OVERCOME
No temptation has seized you except what is common to man.
And God is faithful; he will not let you be tempted beyond
what you can bear. But when you are tempted, he will also
provide a way out so that you can stand up under it.
                                          1 Corinthians 10:13

You will never face a temptation that cannot be overcome with the help of God. That is comforting, but it is
also challenging because it removes all excuses. No longer
are you able to say, "I can't help it." God says you *can*

quit drinking, you *can* break off the relationship, you can quit lusting, you *can* control your temper. The Bible gives two simple keys to overcoming temptation.

1. Flee from temptation. The Bible commands us to flee from our sinful desires. We are warned to flee from
- sexual immorality (1 Corinthians 6:18).
- idolatry (1 Corinthians 10:14).
- the love of money (1 Timothy 6:11).
- the evil desires of youth (2 Timothy 2:22).

When Potiphar's wife was trying to seduce Joseph, he didn't say to himself, "I'm strong enough to resist this temptation, so I'll stay for a while since I'm enjoying the company." He literally ran out of the house (Genesis 39:12). Today we don't consider him a wimp because he ran away, but one of the strongest characters of the Old Testament because he maintained his integrity.

Sometimes parents say they won't guard their kids from certain temptations because they want them to know what the "real world" is like. But Christians are to be "innocent about what is evil" (Romans 16:19; see also 1 Corinthians 14:20). You do not learn to resist temptation by toying with it. Flirting with temptation is like playing with fire. Flee from temptation.

2. Fight temptation. When we do face temptation, as we inevitably will, we must realize that we are fighting a spiritual battle and equip ourselves accordingly by "putting on the full armor of God." With God's help, temptation can be overcome.

Finally, be strong in the Lord and in his mighty power. Put on the full armor of God so that you can take your stand against the devil's schemes. For our struggle is not against flesh and blood, but against the rulers, against the authorities, against the powers of this dark world and against the spiritual forces of evil in the heavenly realms. Therefore put on the full armor of God, so that when the day of evil comes, you may be able to stand your ground, and after you have done every- thing, to stand. Stand firm then, with the belt of truth buck- led around your waist, with the breastplate of righteousness in place, and with your feet fitted with the readiness that comes from the gospel of peace. In addition to all this, take up the shield of faith, with which you can extinguish all the flaming arrows of the evil one. Take the helmet of salvation and the sword of the Spirit, which is the word of God. And pray in the Spirit on all occasions with all kinds of prayers and re- quests.   *Ephesians 6:10-18*

The battle against temptation is never finished as long as we live on this earth. A Catholic priest was asked to describe the point in his life when he felt he had con- quered the desires of the flesh. He said, "I wouldn't trust my flesh until it had been dead at least three days." But when we submit to Christ, sin no longer reigns in us. Christ gives us the power to overcome.

For we know that our old self was crucified with him so that the body of sin might be done away with, that we should no longer be slaves to sin—because anyone who has died has been freed from sin. . . . For sin shall not be your master, because you are not under law, but under grace.   *Romans 6:6, 7, 14*

You will face temptation, and you will sometimes fall. But how much better when we do not fall! God promises a way out if you will trust in Him. You can win the bat- tles against temptation with God's help. Christ alone can keep you from falling!

To him who is able to keep <u>*you*</u> <u>*from*</u> <u>*falling*</u> *and to present you before his glorious presence without fault and with great joy—to the only God our Savior be glory, majesty, power and authority, through Jesus Christ our Lord.*   *Jude 24, 25*

So I say, live by the Spirit, and you will not gratify the desires of the sinful nature.   *Galatians 5:16*

The one who is in you is greater than the one who is in the world.   *1 John 4:4*

Submit yourselves, then, to God. Resist the devil, and he will flee from you.   *James 4:7*

The God of peace will soon crush Satan under your feet.
                    Romans 16:20

IN TIMES OF REBELLION

Jonah 1–4

"Question Authority!" Those aren't just words you will see on a bumper sticker. They have become the motto of a generation. No longer is the voice of the parent the authority in the home. No longer is the voice of the teacher the authority in the classroom. There is no longer respect for a policeman on a street corner or an elderly person in the neighborhood.

When was the last time you heard a young person say, "Yes, sir," or "No, ma'am"? This is a talk-back, fight-back, get-back generation. Instead of a teachable spirit and humble attitude, our society is full of people with a curled lip and defiant look, warning, "Don't tell me what to do."

I talked with a teacher who quit teaching a few years ago. She said, "I love to teach, but I got tired of spending thirty-five minutes disciplining and fifteen minutes teaching. I didn't want to be a glorified rent-a-cop in the classroom."

Church kids don't seem to be doing much better. A 1994 survey by the Barna Research Group revealed the following about kids who attend church, believe their parents love them, and feel their home life is positive:

- Two out of three admitted lying to their parents or

teachers. One out of three had cheated on an exam in the last three months.

- One in nine had gotten drunk, one in ten had used illegal drugs, one in five had tried to physically hurt another person.
- Forty percent didn't believe their faith could be objectively shown to be true, feeling that "no one can prove which religion is absolutely true."
- Twenty-one percent believed that Muslims, Buddhists, Christians, and Jews all pray to the same God, even if they use different names for God.
- Fifty-five percent admitted they had been sexually involved with another teenager.

Rebellion against authority, even God's authority, is common. Maybe you have been praying for a son or daughter, a friend, or maybe even a parent, who has rebelled against God. Perhaps you yourself are searching. You know you've been running from God, and this chapter caught your eye for a good reason. Maybe you're facing temptation right now and you must choose whether you will run to God or away from God. In this chapter we will discuss some surprising and encouraging promises from God during times of rebellion.

First, let's study the Old Testament account of the prophet Jonah, a man who went through a time of rebellion against God.

JONAH'S REBELLION

The word of the Lord came to Jonah son of Amittai: "Go to the great city of Nineveh and preach against it, because its wickedness has come up before me."   Jonah 1:1, 2

You may wonder why any prophet who directly hears the voice of God wouldn't do what God asked him to do. We think, "Surely if I heard God's voice, I would go wherever He wanted me to go!" But Nineveh was not the place you would want to go to preach. You especially wouldn't want to "preach against it"—tell the people of Nineveh exactly what God thought of their wickedness— as God had commanded. The Ninevites were barbarians. They had been at war with the Israelites and had conquered Jonah's hometown. They may have even killed Jonah's parents or other relatives. And they were famous for their cruel torture of prisoners of war. Nineveh's torture tactics against Jewish slaves were even more horrible than those of the Nazis. No one would want to go to Nineveh, especially if he were of Jewish descent as Jonah was.

Some of my close relatives decided to go to Japan as missionaries shortly after World War II. It was the right thing for them to do, but it must have been difficult to minister to the people who had bombed Pearl Harbor just a few years earlier. Jonah was commanded to go directly into the enemy camp—while they were still enemies.

But Jonah ran away from the Lord and headed for Tarshish. He went down to Joppa, where he found a ship bound for that port. After paying the fare, he went aboard and sailed for Tarshish to flee from the Lord.   Jonah 1:3

I can sympathize with Jonah's desire to run away. Shortly before my wife and I went on a short-term mission trip to Kenya, Africa, it was reported that there had been several instances of violence against tourists near the area we were supposed to be visiting. The natives had attacked and robbed the tourists, even killing one tour guide. When it came time for us to go to Kenya, I wanted to go to Hawaii instead! Certainly they need the Lord in Hawaii, too!

You would expect God to immediately block the way when Jonah ran the other direction. But Jonah didn't encounter roadblocks in his flight away from God. He had no trouble finding a ship ready to leave for Tarshish. He had enough money to pay the fare. He was even able to find a comfortable place below deck to lie down—and he fell asleep! (See Jonah 1:5.)

God probably gave Jonah some warning signals. He surely felt some remorse, though he hid it well. He probably had difficulty telling his family and friends where he was going or when he would be back. But things went relatively smoothly for Jonah at first.

I have counseled many men who have been unfaithful to their wives. Often they express how easy it was to fall. There were chance meetings and coincidental rendezvous; there were feelings of companionship and oneness. The apparent "open doors" allowed them to rationalize that it must be the Lord's will for them to enter this new relationship. They were experiencing smooth sailing, but they were headed in the wrong direction!

JONAH'S REPENTANCE

Jonah probably rationalized at first that he would preach to the people in Tarshish, and perhaps God would think that was sufficient. Or maybe he really believed that if he ran far enough, to a desolate enough place, he could hide from God. But Jonah hadn't run from God at all. God loved Jonah too much to let him get by with his rebellion. God set a series of events in motion to wake Jonah from his physical sleep and his spiritual slumber.

Then the Lord sent a great wind on the sea, and such a violent storm arose that the ship threatened to break up. All the sailors were afraid and each cried out to his own god. And they threw the cargo into the sea to lighten the ship.

Jonah 1:4, 5

A storm arose, strong enough to terrify even the experienced sailors on the ship. But Jonah slept through the storm! The sailors shook him awake and told him to start praying to his God as they had been praying to their gods, in hopes that someone's God would save them.

They decided to cast lots to determine which among them had sinned to cause the "gods" to mistreat them. Proverbs 16:33 reads, "The lot is cast into the lap, but its every decision is from the Lord." Christians should depend on the Word of God and the Holy Spirit for direction, not the casting of lots. But God can use any means He wants to see that His plan succeeds. The lot fell to Jonah. Then it was question-and-answer time.

So they asked him, "Tell us, who is responsible for making all this trouble for us? What do you do? Where do you come from? What is your country? From what people are you?"
                                                                    Jonah 1:8

When he was confronted, Jonah confessed his sin.

He answered, "I am a Hebrew and I worship the Lord, the God of heaven, who made the sea and the land."   *Jonah 1:9*

Admitting your sinfulness is the first necessary step toward repentance. Jonah told them he was running from the Lord. As the storm got rougher, he said they would be saved only if they threw him overboard. He probably didn't expect God to save him. He thought he was about to die. But his heart was softening, and he cared about the others on board. There was no reason for them to die, too, because of his disobedience.

The men tried to row back to land, but they couldn't. Finally, after praying to Jonah's God for mercy, they threw Jonah overboard. The sea grew calm.

At this the men greatly feared the Lord, and they offered a sacrifice to the Lord and made vows to him.   *Jonah 1:16*

God can use even our periods of rebellion for His glory. He will work all things out for His good. There are always painful consequences to our rebellion, and Jonah would pay dearly for his disobedience. But just as God used Jonah's period of rebellion to witness to some pagan sailors, God can turn our disobedience into something that brings honor to Him.

But the Lord provided a great fish to swallow Jonah, and Jonah was inside the fish three days and three nights.
Jonah 1:17

People often scoff at the idea that a man could live inside a fish for three days. But I believe this story literally happened for several reasons.

It is part of God's inspired Word. It is not told as a parable or an allegory, but as a true story with real people and real places. If God created the world, He could create a fish for this special purpose. The Scripture doesn't say it was a whale, but a fish, that swallowed Jonah. If man can create a submarine and live in it under water for months, surely God can create a fish that could house Jonah for three days.

Jesus spoke of the story as if it were true. Jesus said, "For as Jonah was three days and three nights in the belly of a huge fish, so the Son of Man will be three days and three nights in the heart of the earth" (Matthew 12:40). The problem with choosing parts of the Bible to believe and parts to discard is that they are all related. If the story of Jonah is a myth, Jesus either did not know what He was talking about, or He deceived his listeners on purpose. Either option destroys the deity of Jesus.

Jonah wrote an accurate account of the incident. Jonah described in great detail what it was like to be "hurled into the deep" (Jonah 2:3-5), to "the roots of the mountains" (Jonah 2:3-6). It wasn't until recent years that we discovered there are mountains under the sea! How did Jonah know unless he had been there?

Three days in the belly of a fish had a way of making Jonah think. He repented before God and asked for a second chance. He wrote about his experience:

"In my distress I called to the Lord,
* and he answered me.*
From the depths of the grave I called for help,
* and you listened to my cry.*
You hurled me into the deep,
* into the very heart of the seas,*
* and the currents swirled about me;*
all your waves and breakers
* swept over me.*
I said, 'I have been banished
* from your sight;*
yet I will look again
* toward your holy temple.'"*   *Jonah 2:2-4*

Sometimes when loved ones rebel, we pray that God might protect them. We can see they are running down a dangerous path away from God, and we don't want them to suffer. We pray that God might be merciful and bring them back without suffering.

But God may have a different plan in mind. The rebellious person may need pain or conflict—maybe poverty, a broken relationship, loneliness, or physical hardship—to arouse him from his spiritual slumber. Maybe our prayer should be, "Lord, whatever it takes to bring him back to you, please do it. I want his soul to be saved." God has often used financial failure, an accident, illness, a broken marriage, the death of a child, or the loss of a job to turn people from their rebellion.

Jonah's prayer reveals he was thankful for his harsh

experience that brought him back to God.

"When my life was ebbing away,
  I remembered you, Lord,
and my prayer rose to you,
  to your holy temple.

"Those who cling to worthless idols
  forfeit the grace that could be theirs.
But I, with a song of thanksgiving,
  will sacrifice to you.
What I have vowed I will make good.
  Salvation comes from the Lord."   *Jonah 2:7-9*

JONAH'S RESTORATION

  And the Lord commanded the fish, and it vomited Jonah onto dry land.
  Then the word of the Lord came to Jonah a second time: "Go to the great city of Nineveh and proclaim to it the message I give you."   *Jonah 2:10–3:2*

God offered Jonah a second chance. And God's second command sounded very similar to the first! He didn't change His mind or meet Jonah in the middle. He still commanded Jonah to go to Nineveh. God's Word doesn't change. When He issues a command, it isn't up for bargaining. James 1:17 declares, "[God] does not change like shifting shadows."

I sometimes imagine that Jonah, when he was spit out onto the beach, looked up and saw a sign that read, "Nineveh Highway, three miles ahead." This time Jonah decided to obey.

  Jonah obeyed the word of the Lord and went to Nineveh. Now Nineveh was a very important city–a visit required three days.   *Jonah 3:3*

NINEVEH'S RESPONSE

As Jonah went through the streets of Nineveh, a town of more than 120,000 people, he must have drawn a crowd wherever he went! He proclaimed God's message: "Forty more days and Nineveh will be overturned" (3:4).

Jonah apparently took delight in preaching of the destruction of the city. After all the Ninevites had done to his people, it probably felt good to tell them exactly how God would punish them. But a strange thing happened. The people—from the peasants to the king—listened to Jonah. Another reason I believe in the literal account of Jonah is the reaction of the Ninevites in the third chapter of the book of Jonah. I think those hardened people repented to God at the sight of Jonah! He must have looked disgusting. His skin and hair probably had been eaten away by the enzymes of the fish. He probably smelled awful, too! When he told them where he had been, they believed him! The whole town wept before God and repented of their sins.

The Ninevites believed God. They declared a fast, and all of them, from the greatest to the least, put on sackcloth.
                                                                    Jonah 3:5

Even the king repented in sackcloth and ashes and decreed to the town that everyone call upon God for mercy. "Who knows?" the king said. "God may yet relent and with compassion turn from his fierce anger so that we will not perish" (Jonah 3:9). The entire city of Nineveh repented, changed their wicked ways, and prayed to God for mercy.

When God saw what they did and how they turned from their evil ways, he had compassion and did not bring upon them the destruction he had threatened.   *Jonah 3:10*

JONAH'S REGRET
But Jonah was greatly displeased and became angry.

Jonah 4:1

Jonah had a surprising response to all this. He got angry with God for not destroying the city. He was livid that the Ninevites were not getting what they deserved. Jonah said, "See, Lord, that's why I didn't want to go to Nineveh! I knew You wouldn't really destroy them—You are too compassionate. They will never get what they really deserve" (Jonah 4:1, 2, my paraphrase). Anger makes us say some stupid things. Jonah tried to blame his disobedience on God's compassion!

Maybe Jonah was also angry because his reputation was tarnished. He had bravely promised everyone that God was going to destroy the city of Nineveh. What would people think of him if the city was spared? But God explained to Jonah that he had no right to be angry. The people of Nineveh were more important to God than Jonah's reputation. The city was spared.

PROMISES FOR THOSE WHO REBEL

Not all of God's promises are comforting! You might expect me to write about God's compassion and patience with those who rebel, His desire to forgive, and His constant watch over you. It's true that God promises those things. But God promises one thing first: discipline.

DISCIPLINE FOR THE REBELLIOUS

If you have declared yourself to be a child of God, you can expect God to treat you like one of His children. You cannot run away from God. You really wouldn't want to be able to run from God. In the end you will be glad that you couldn't go so far or so low that He could not find you. Consider this passage about the Lord's discipline:

"My son, do not make light of the Lord's discipline,
and do not lose heart when he rebukes you,
because the Lord disciplines those he loves,
and he punishes everyone he accepts as a son."
Endure hardship as discipline; God is treating you as sons.
For what son is not disciplined by his father?. . . Our fathers
disciplined us for a little while as they thought best; but God
disciplines us for our good, that we may share in his holiness.
No discipline seems pleasant at the time, but painful. Later
on, however, it produces a harvest of righteousness and peace
for those who have been trained by it.   Hebrews 12:5-7, 11

Rebellion inevitably results in discipline, because God loves us. A loving father may spank a son who continues to walk out into a dangerous street against the father's commands. The father wants his son to feel a little pain in order to avoid worse pain—or even death. It is the same in our relationship with the heavenly Father.

The purpose of God's discipline is not to punish or hurt us, but to produce repentance. The writer of Hebrews called it, "A harvest of righteousness and peace" (Hebrews 12:11). God loves us too much to let us go without making an attempt to bring us back.

I heard about a little boy, Joey, who was playing with a slingshot. He got carried away and shot a rock at his grandmother's pet duck. He didn't expect to be so accurate, but he hit and killed the duck. His sister Sally saw him and threatened to tell Grandma unless Joey did exactly as she instructed.

That night after supper Grandma said, "Sally, will you please help with the dishes?"

Sally said, "Oh, Joey said he would help with the dishes tonight, right Joey?" Then she whispered to him, "Remember the duck." Joey cleaned the dishes.

Later Grandpa said, "Sally and Joey, would you like to go fishing with me in the morning?"

"I need someone to stay here and help me dust the furniture," said Grandma.

"Oh, Joey said he would stay, right Joey?" Sally grinned. Then she whispered, "Remember the duck."

The pattern continued for several days, Joey doing all of Sally's chores and Sally enjoying herself very much, until Joey had all he could take. He went to his grandmother and confessed to shooting the duck.

"I know you did," said Grandma. "I was watching from the kitchen window. Because I love you, I forgave you. I just wanted to see how long you would let Sally make a slave out of you."

Sin enslaves us and destroys our freedom. But God may allow us to suffer the natural consequences of our sin, especially rebellious sin, that we might turn to Him in repentance and gain freedom from the bondage of sin.

RESTORATION FOR THE REPENTANT

God hates sin. One of the sins he hates the most is a rebellious spirit—someone who pretends to sacrifice for God, but in his heart is leading a defiant, disobedient lifestyle. He created the worst place imaginable—hell—for Satan when he rebelled against God. When King Saul rebelled, Samuel had some harsh words from God for him:

> *But Samuel replied:*
> *"Does the Lord delight in burnt offerings and sacrifices*
>   *as much as in obeying the voice of the Lord?*
> *To obey is better than sacrifice*
>   *and to heed is better than the fat of rams.*
> *For rebellion is like the sin of divination,*
>   *and arrogance like the evil of idolatry.*
> *Because you have rejected the word of the Lord,*
>   *he has rejected you as king."*   *1 Samuel 15:22, 23*

But God loves the sinner even more strongly than He

hates the sin. He sacrificed His own innocent Son to save the rebellious. And He promises that even now, no matter how far you have run from Him, if you repent God will restore you.

"'Return, faithless Israel,' declares the Lord,
'I will frown on you no longer,
for I am merciful,' declares the Lord,
'I will not be angry forever.
Only acknowledge your guilt—
you have rebelled against the Lord your God,
you have scattered your favors to foreign gods
under every spreading tree,
and have not obeyed me,'"
declares the Lord. Jeremiah 3:12, 13

"Return, faithless people; I will cure you of backsliding."
Jeremiah 3:22

[God said], "If my people, who are called by my name, will humble themselves and pray and seek my face and turn from their wicked ways, then will I hear from heaven and will forgive their sin and will heal their land." 2 Chronicles 7:14

To illustrate God's willingness to forgive the rebellious, Jesus told a story about a son who shamelessly took his share of his father's wealth and rode off to a far country to waste it on riotous living. When the son was left with nothing, he was humbled and wanted to come home. He rationalized that his father's hired hands had it better than he; perhaps his father would hire him as a servant, since he certainly was not worthy to be a son.

The son headed for home, expecting to find an angry father to whom he would have to repent. He memorized his speech on the way home. "I am not worthy to be called your son," he kept practicing. "May I just be one of the servants that I might live here under your care?"

"But while he was still a long way off, his father saw him and was filled with compassion for him; he ran to his son, threw his arms around him and kissed him."　　*Luke 15:20*

It's the only time in Scripture that God is pictured as being in a hurry—running to forgive His rebellious son who has repented. The father muffled his son's repentant speech in his chest as he hugged him to himself. Jesus continued:

"But the father said to his servants, 'Quick! Bring the best robe and put it on him. Put a ring on his finger and sandals on his feet. Bring the fattened calf and kill it. Let's have a feast and celebrate. For this son of mine was dead and is alive again; he was lost and is found.' So they began to celebrate."

Luke 15:22-24

The greatest part of God's restoration is that it is complete and whole. In fact, it inevitably leads to *increased responsibility* in the kingdom.

- Jonah was restored, but he still had to go to Nineveh.
- King David, when he repented from his adultery, asked to be restored, saying, "Then I will teach transgressors your ways." (Psalm 51:13). He knew he would have added responsibilities when he was forgiven.
- Simon Peter was forgiven after denying Jesus, but then Jesus commanded Peter, "Feed my sheep" (John 21:17). A restored Simon Peter became the leader of the first-century church.

A friend of mine was an elder in his church when he began a terrible habit of gambling. His habit grew so bad that he started embezzling from his company to pay for his debts. Eventually, to the horror of his family, he was caught and jailed for his behavior. But when his sin was

disclosed, he repented before God and longed to be restored. After serving his time in jail, he humbly and patiently took a behind-the-scenes role in his church.
Several years went by, but he remained faithful. Then he felt God's call to enter the ministry. He left his job and began working full-time in the church where he had been serving behind the scenes. Today he has a vibrant ministry for Christ.

Though God's grace is sufficient to restore the rebellious, we must remember that rebellion, like any sin, leaves a scar. Jonah's flesh and hair were probably never the same again—a constant reminder of his rebellion. King David lost a son and nearly destroyed his family because of his rebellion. Peter had to live with the painful memory that he had denied the Christ.

Harry Emerson Fosdick said, "There is one thing better than bringing home the prodigal son from the far country. That is keeping the son home in the first place, in a right relationship with the father." We all have sinned, but not everyone rebels against God by running away in direct defiance to His call. If you have rebelled, it is time to repent and come home to the Father. If you are in a right relationship with God, remember you are not invincible. Remind yourself, "There, but for the grace of God, go I." Walk daily with the Lord, be obedient, and thank Him for His grace in your life.

For you were once darkness, but now you are light in the Lord. Live as children of light.   *Ephesians 5:8*

IN TIMES OF GUILT

Matthew 3:1-17; 27:45-56

The United States government has had a "conscience fund" for many years to provide relief for people who feel guilty about cheating the government. Thousands of letters and millions of dollars have been anonymously mailed to the fund over the years.

- In 1974 someone wrote, "I am sending ten dollars for the blanket I stole while I was in World War II. My mind could not rest. I am sorry I'm late." It was signed, "An Ex-GI." He concluded, "P.S. I want to be ready to meet God."
- A Colorado woman sent in two eight-cent stamps to make up for having used one stamp twice when it hadn't been canceled the first time.
- A former IRS employee mailed in one dollar for four ballpoint pens she had never returned to her office.
- A man from Salem, Ohio, submitted one dollar with the following note, "When I was a boy, I put a few pennies on the railroad track and the train flattened them. I also used a dime in a silver-coating experiment in high school. I understand there is a law against defacing money. I have not seen it but I desire to be a law-abiding citizen."

- One man sent in $150, admitting that he had
  cheated on his income taxes. His letter concluded,
  "If I still can't sleep, I'll send the rest later."

We all know what it means to feel guilty. Maybe it's as
simple as knowing you should have returned the ballpoint pens. Maybe the guilt is over a more serious offense: broken promises, stolen property, wounded
relationships, exploited people, abused bodies.

Today's pop psychologists don't like the emotion of
guilt. They will do what they can to convince you that
your guilty emotions are misplaced, that you should learn
to forgive yourself for your past mistakes and feel good
about who you are. "Concentrate on the good things you
have done," they'll say. "Make the effort to heal a relationship if necessary, but don't beat yourself up over it.
It surely was not all your fault anyway."

Dr. James Dobson tells of a young man who was hired
by his neighbors to watch their house while they were
gone on vacation. The couple gave the fifteen year old a
key to the house and asked him to water the lawn, bring
in the mail, and maintain the property until they returned. The young man did his job and was paid for his
efforts.

But some months later he knocked on their front
door. When they invited him in, he stood in the door-
way, obviously shaken with emotion, saying he had something important to tell them. They sat him down in their
living room, where he confessed to the couple that he
had entered the house one day to bring in the mail and
had seen a stick of gum lying on the table. He had stolen
the gum and chewed it, but had suffered intense guilt
ever since.

The young man, weeping, took a penny from his
pocket and asked them to accept it as repayment for the
stolen gum, requesting forgiveness for his dishonesty.

If you were counseling that sensitive young man about how to handle his guilt, what would you have told him? Should he have not felt so guilty over such a minor thing? Would you have said, "Look, they probably wouldn't have cared anyway. Just ask God's forgiveness and go on"? Or would you have counseled him to confess and make recompense as he did?

In a study about guilt, it's important that we understand the biblical view of the conscience. Our conscience is the part inside of us that makes us feel guilty at times. One Christian counselor said, "Guilt is a message of disapproval from the conscience which says in effect, 'You should be ashamed of yourself.'"

Though our conscience is an important part of the emotional make-up that God has given us, our conscience is not always reliable. Jiminy Cricket's advice to "let your conscience be your guide" is not always wise advice.

Weak Conscience

The Bible mentions four types of conscience. The first is a *weak* conscience. Sometimes people feel guilty when they should not. Paul wrote to the Corinthians about the debate over food that had been sacrificed to idols. Meat that had been sacrificed to idols was evidently sold in the marketplace at a discount. Christians debated about whether it was acceptable to eat such meat.

Paul explained that an idol is nothing at all; we ought to have the freedom to eat the meat if we want. Then he wrote:

> *But not everyone knows this. Some people are still so accustomed to idols that when they eat such food they think of it as having been sacrificed to an idol, and since their <u>conscience is weak</u>, it is defiled.*
>
> *1 Corinthians 8:7, emphasis added*

People often feel guilty about things that aren't sins. One mother might feel guilty if her house isn't spotless. A young couple might feel guilty if they have nicer things than most couples. Some adult children are made to feel guilty by their parents for not visiting as often as the parents would like. You may feel guilty if you don't say yes to every request for volunteers at church. I know of Christians who feel guilty if they listen to music with drums in it, or if they drink a soft drink with caffeine in it.

I used to feel guilty if I was not working all the time. I could hardly enjoy a day of vacation. I even felt guilty if I got a call at 3:00 A.M. and I was asleep! I'd clear my throat, pick up the phone and say hello as clearly as I could, as though I'd been up praying, just waiting for the phone to ring!

SEARED CONSCIENCE

A more common misuse of our conscience is what the Bible calls a *seared* conscience. Paul warned Timothy about false teachings:

"Such teachings come through hypocritical liars, whose <u>consciences</u> <u>have</u> <u>been</u> <u>seared</u> as with a hot iron."

1 Timothy 4:2, emphasis added

If you habitually violate your conscience, it will become seared. A Canadian Indian pictured his conscience as "a little three-cornered thing inside my heart. When I do wrong," he said, "it turns around and hurts me very much. But if I keep on doing wrong, it will turn so much that the corners become worn off and it doesn't hurt anymore."

Often the most effective silencer for the conscience is majority opinion. If everybody is doing it, or at least no one sees anything wrong with it, we don't feel guilty about going along. Our conscience can become seared very quickly. That explains why many young people today can feel no remorse over having sexual relations with someone they feel they "love," without any commitment. Thirty years ago teenagers felt guilty about such behavior. But now that it is socially acceptable, it's much easier to ignore any feelings of guilt, rationalize the behavior, and sear the conscience.

Our conscience is like a computer. It spits out whatever has been programmed into it. If we feed it the wrong information, it will alarm us at the wrong times. That's why it is so important that we continue to study the Word of God, which never changes. His standards of morality are eternal and are not open for negotiation. His laws will remain even if the whole world rejects them. That's why the psalmist wrote, "I have hidden your word in my heart that I might not sin against you" (Psalm 119:11). Jiminy Cricket should have said, "Let God's Word be your guide."

GUILTY CONSCIENCE

Let us draw near to God with a sincere heart in full assurance of faith, having our hearts sprinkled to cleanse us from a guilty conscience and having our bodies washed with pure water.   *Hebrews 10:22, emphasis added*

The first two types of conscience are wrongly programmed. The person with a weak conscience feels guilty when he shouldn't. The other, with a seared conscience, doesn't feel guilty when he should. There is a third type of conscience I can only describe as a *guilty* conscience. I refer to the person who feels guilty, but rightfully so. His conscience is bothering him because it *should* bother him. There are times when you should feel guilty, because you *are* guilty.

Whether you feel guilty or not, there are times when you are guilty. A person who robs a bank should feel a sense of guilt after his action. But whether he feels guilty or not does not change the truth. He is guilty of breaking the law. If justice is served, the jury will render a verdict of *guilty*. He can plead all he wants that he does not *feel* guilty. It doesn't matter, because he *is* guilty.

A conscience rightly programmed by the Word of God will cause you to feel guilty when you do something that violates God's commands. It is a positive emotion that makes you realize you are a sinner in need of God's forgiveness. Until we face that reality and receive God's forgiveness, we should feel a sense of guilt because we *are* guilty before God.

As it is written:
  "There is no one righteous, not even one;
    there is no one who understands,
    no one who seeks God.
  All have turned away,
    they have together become worthless;
  there is no one who does good,
    not even one."   *Romans 3:10-12*

For all have sinned and fall short of the glory of God.
                                                  Romans 3:23

CLEAR CONSCIENCE
The fourth type of conscience is a *clear* conscience.

But do this with gentleness and respect, keeping <u>a clear conscience</u>, so that those who speak maliciously against your good behavior in Christ may be ashamed of their slander.
                          1 Peter 3:15, 16, emphasis added

A clear conscience is one that feels clean because it is clean. There are two ways to get a clear conscience:

You can be without sin. Only Jesus lived a perfect life, so only Jesus had the right to a "clear conscience" under this first scenario.

You can be forgiven of your sin. It may seem like a minor offense, but the boy who stole the piece of gum did steal and violated the character of God who would not steal. Therefore, he needed to be forgiven of his sin. Since we have all broken at least one of God's commands, we do not have the right to a clear conscience until we have been forgiven by God.

How do you get a clear conscience? You must understand and accept God's promises about your guilt and His grace.

PROMISES TO THE GUILTY

The Bible is not a single book, but a compilation of sixty-six books spanning a period of fifteen hundred years in history. The Bible is an inspired work of history, revealing God's loving relationship with man. Someone said the Bible could be divided into three parts: God creates man (Genesis 1-2); man falls from God's grace (Genesis 3); and God redeems man to himself (the rest of the Bible). In that span of history, God promises several things that relate to our guilt before Him and His desire to redeem us.

GOD PROMISES A SAVIOR

God promised a Savior from the time man first sinned. God had promised Adam and Eve they could live in the perfect Garden of Eden as long as they were obedient. If they disobeyed, they would die. When Eve ate from the tree of knowledge of good and evil, then convinced her husband Adam to do the same, guilt resulted. Adam and Eve *felt* guilty for the first time. They

noticed that they were naked. They were no longer innocent. They hid from God. They felt guilty because they
were guilty.

God banished Adam and Eve from the paradise He
had created for them, and the death process began. But
God was not finished with man. There are two clues in
Genesis 3 that lead us to a promised plan of redemption.

The first clue can be seen in the curse of the serpent
that deceived Eve.

> *So the Lord God said to the serpent, "Because you have*
> *done this,*
> *"Cursed are you above all the livestock*
> *and all the wild animals!*
> *You will crawl on your belly*
> *and you will eat dust*
> *all the days of your life.*
> *And I will put enmity*
> *between you and the woman,*
> *and between your offspring and hers;*
> *he will crush your head,*
> *and you will strike his heel."* Genesis 3:14, 15

The indication that the woman's offspring would
"crush the head" of the serpent and yet the serpent
would "strike his heel" was a prophecy of the death of
Jesus, which would be the moment in time that sin was
conquered.

The second clue came following the curse of Adam
and Eve. When God removed them from the garden, He
made clothes for the man and woman out of animal
skin. God gave them new clothes, not because He felt
their garments of fig leaves were indecent, but because
He was beginning to illustrate that sin required the shed-
ding of blood.

God promised a Savior through the Law. Throughout the Old Testament, the Lord illustrated that sin meant death. The Israelites were required to kill an innocent lamb to pay for their sins. God was conditioning the people that sin meant death. Yet they knew that their sacrifices did not completely remove sin.

The law is only a shadow of the good things that are coming—not the realities themselves. For this reason it can never, by the same sacrifices repeated endlessly year after year, make perfect those who draw near to worship. If it could, would they not have stopped being offered? For the worshipers would have been cleansed once for all, and would no longer have felt guilty for their sins. But those sacrifices are an annual reminder of sins, because it is impossible for the blood of bulls and goats to take away sins. Hebrews 10:1-4

God promised a Savior through the Old Testament prophets. Hundreds of years before Jesus was born, Isaiah wrote in a poetic past tense about the coming Messiah:

Surely he took up our infirmities
and carried our sorrows,
yet we considered him stricken by God, `
smitten by him, and afflicted.
But he was pierced for our transgressions,
he was crushed for our iniquities;
the punishment that brought us peace was upon
him,
and by his wounds we are healed.
We all, like sheep, have gone astray,
each of us has turned to his own way;
and the Lord has laid on him
the iniquity of us all. Isaiah 53:4-6

Jeremiah wrote directly of God's promise to man, regarding the coming Messiah:

"No longer will a man teach his neighbor,
  or a man his brother, saying, 'Know the Lord,'
because they will all know me,
    from the least of them to the greatest,"
      declares the Lord.
"For I will forgive their wickedness
    and will remember their sins no more."   Jeremiah 31:34

Jesus Christ was the fulfillment of God's promise of a Savior. When John the Baptist was preaching in the desert of Judea, prophesying that the kingdom of Heaven was near, Jesus came to John to be baptized. John said, "Look, the Lamb of God, who takes away the sin of the world!" (John 1:29).

At first John the Baptist claimed he wasn't worthy to baptize Jesus. But Jesus said, "Let it be so now; it is proper for us to do this to fulfill all righteousness" (Matthew 3:15). Jesus didn't need to be baptized, because He was sinless. He did it out of obedience, to set an example, and to show that a new covenant was beginning—a new relationship between God and man.

GOD PROMISES FORGIVENESS OF SINS

Jesus had come to die for the sins of the world. God could not allow sin to go unpunished, but He would accept the substitutionary death of one righteous Man for the sins of unrighteous man. Only one could fulfill that requirement because only one had lived a sinless life: the perfect man Jesus Christ.

For all have sinned and fall short of the glory of God, and are justified freely by his grace through the redemption that came by Christ Jesus. God presented him as a sacrifice of atonement through faith in his blood. He did this to demonstrate his justice, because in his forbearance he had left the sins committed beforehand unpunished.   Romans 3:23-25

In Charles Dickens's *A Tale of Two Cities,* the young Frenchman Charles Darnay was condemned to die by the guillotine. When Sidney Carton learned of the plight of his friend, he determined to save him by laying down his own life in the place of Darnay. He was willing to do it, not for the love he had for his friend, but for the sake of Darnay's wife and child.

The night before Darnay's execution, Sidney Carton gained admission to the dungeon and changed garments with the condemned man. The next day he was put to death as Charles Darnay. Before he died he said, "'Tis a far, far better thing that I do than I have ever done."

That's what Jesus did for us. He put on our soiled garments of sin and was led to the cross to experience the punishment we deserved. He suffered the most excruciating death imaginable to pay the price for our sin. Isaiah had prophesied correctly: "The Lord has laid on him the iniquity of us all" (Isaiah 53:6).

Just as Charles Darnay was freed from death, we are freed from sin and death as well through the blood of Christ. God promises us freedom from sin if we will accept Christ's substitutionary death for us. What a great promise! Once we have trusted in Christ's saving grace, we don't have to feel guilty, because we *aren't* guilty anymore!

Therefore, there is now no condemnation for those who are in Christ Jesus.   *Romans 8:1*

If we confess our sins, he is faithful and just and will forgive us our sins and purify us from all unrighteousness.
                                                                    1 John 1:9

Even when we understand this great promise, it's sometimes difficult to believe God could really forgive our sins. "You don't know what I've done," someone will say, "There is no way God could forgive me." But to make that claim is to show a lack of faith in the promise of God. He knows what you did. He knew what you were going to do when He made those promises. He paid for your sin on the cross. The Bible gives at least five wonderful illustrations of how God removes our sins from us when He forgives us.

1. God Removes Our Sins as Far as East From West!

For as high as the heavens are above the earth,
so great is his love for those who fear him;
as far as the east is from the west,
so far has he removed our transgressions
from us. Psalm 103:11, 12

2. God Makes Our "Scarlet" Sins White As Snow!

"Come now, let us reason together,"
says the Lord.
"Though your sins are like scarlet,
they shall be as white as snow;
though they are red as crimson,
they shall be like wool." Isaiah 1:18

3. God Forgets!

This is what the Lord says—
your Redeemer, the Holy One of Israel: . . .
"I, even I, am he who blots out
your transgressions, for my own sake,
and remembers your sins no more." Isaiah 43:14, 25

4. Our Sins Disappear Like The Morning Dew!

"This is what the Lord says—. . .
I have swept away your offenses like a cloud,
your sins like the morning mist.
Return to me,
for I have redeemed you." Isaiah 44:6, 22

5. God Buries Our Sins In The Depths Of The Sea!

Who is a God like you,
who pardons sin and forgives the transgression
of the remnant of his inheritance?
You do not stay angry forever
but delight to show mercy.
You will again have compassion on us;
you will tread our sins underfoot
and hurl all our iniquities into the depths of the sea.

Micah 7:18, 19

GOD PROMISES FREEDOM FROM THE LAW

Therefore, there is now no condemnation for those who are in
Christ Jesus, because through Christ Jesus the law of the
Spirit of life set me free from the law of sin and death.

Romans 8:1, 2

Through Jesus Christ, God not only promises us freedom from sin, He promises freedom from the law. Because of the sacrifice of Christ, you have a permanent "not guilty" stamp on you. Your sins have already been paid for. Paul said, "You are not under law, but under grace" (Romans 6:14). You are permanently freed from guilt.

As Paul later explains, our freedom does not give us a license to do whatever we please. Christians are not only freed from guilt, we are also freed from sin. We should not let sin reign in us anymore. But how comforting it is to know we are no longer bound by the laws we couldn't keep. We are free to live under the grace of God!

In the first few months of construction of the Golden Gate Bridge, several workers fell to their deaths. Construction was halted while a huge safety net was positioned under the bridge. In the remaining days of the project, only two people fell and no one was hurt. The project was completed with even greater efficiency after the net was in place. The net did not make the workers more careless; it made them more *confident.*

So it is with the net of God's grace. We are no longer bound by the law, afraid of falling at any moment. We are free to serve God with greater efficiency.

GOD PROMISES THE GIFT OF ETERNAL LIFE

The greatest promise God gives to the guilty is the gift of eternal life. Because Jesus not only died but rose from the dead, those who trust in Him will do likewise. See chapter twelve, "In Times of Facing Death," where we discuss more about the glorious life awaiting us when we reach Heaven.

"For God so loved the world that he gave his one and only Son, that whoever believes in him shall not perish but have eternal life. For God did not send his Son into the world to condemn the world, but to save the world through him. Whoever believes in him is not condemned, but whoever does not believe stands condemned already because he has not believed in the name of God's one and only Son."

John 3:16-18

Jesus gave them this answer: "I tell you the truth, . . . whoever hears my word and believes him who sent me has eternal life and will not be condemned; he has crossed over from death to life." *John 5:19, 24*

IN TIMES OF WORRY

Mark 4:35-41

A furious storm came through our city about twenty
years ago. A series of tornadoes cut through Louisville,
Kentucky, where we live, destroying homes, overturning
cars, and taking the roofs off dozens of large buildings.
My family made their way to the basement to avoid the
coming storm. I listened to the radio as a helicopter pilot
described the path of the storm. I could tell by his de-
scription that the storm was north of us and would miss
our home by several miles. I stepped outside and could
see in the distance the storm that contained the tornadoes. A horrendous cloud moved rapidly across the hori-
zon about three miles away, cutting a half-mile swath
through parks, subdivisions, and businesses, leaving massive destruction in its wake.

Since then our town has reacted differently to tornado
warnings. People worry that another destructive tornado
might come ripping through their neighborhood. Some
parents will even race to pick up their children early from
school if the weather is right for a tornado. The kids
aren't any safer at home, but Mom and Dad worry a lot
less. If a tornado warning is given, everyone immediately
seeks shelter, because everybody knows from past experience how serious a tornado can be.

The disciples of Jesus once encountered what Mark calls "a furious squall" on the Sea of Galilee. Still today terrible storms can roll over the mountains onto that massive lake almost instantly, catching even the most experienced boaters by surprise. The squall had the disciples so worried they were sure they would drown. In a panic they woke up Jesus, who had slept through the whole thing! They screamed over the pounding waves,

"Teacher, don't you care if we drown?"
He got up, rebuked the wind and said to the waves, "Quiet!
Be still!" Then the wind died down and it was completely
calm.   *Mark 4:38, 39*

When I was a boy, I loved to listen to my mother tell me stories from the Bible. I remember her telling me this story. I listened intently as she told me about the disciples fighting a furious storm and being so worried they would drown, then waking Jesus up in a panic. She told me about Jesus calming the storm in an instant and making everything immediately still.

When she was finished, I said, "Mom, weren't the disciples dumb to be worried when they knew Jesus was in the boat? God wasn't going to let Jesus drown!"

"That's right, Bobby," my mother said, "and you remember that Jesus is always with you, too."

THE PROBLEM OF WORRY

Almost everyone worries at one time or another, but some people are more inclined to worry than others. According to one survey, women are more than twice as likely as men to experience anxiety disorders, especially between the ages of eighteen and forty-four. I have discovered that worry increases with age, too. Young people are naive and don't really know the dangers that lie ahead, or they think "It can never happen to me." Older people have experienced frightful things and can live in fear of history repeating itself.

Anxiety is so common that people almost consider it to be a natural part of life. But God doesn't want you to worry. I can think of three good reasons why.

WORRY RUINS OUR HEALTH

Doctors have tried to tell us for a long time that worry is hard on the body. Since the Bible calls your body the "temple of the Holy Spirit" (1 Corinthians 6:19), we should want to overcome our anxiety to protect His temple.

At least 50 percent of those with anxiety disorders have been forced to seek medical attention in the past six months. They've asked neurologists to cure their dizzy spells; they've seen gastroenterologists because of digestive disorders; they've visited cardiologists complaining about chest pains; they've seen respiratory specialists about their shortness of breath. Only a fourth of those seeking medical assistance from worry-related illnesses will get help with the source of their problem— their anxiety. Alcohol or substance abuse, depression, sexual disorders, and suicide occur more often among those with anxiety disorders, as do heart disease, high blood pressure, and other circulatory problems.

WORRY MINIMIZES OUR EFFECTIVENESS

When Thomas Carlyle lived in London, his neighbor kept chickens. The rooster disturbed Carlyle's sleep with its loud crowing. When Carlyle complained, the owner protested, "You have no complaint. He only crows three or four times a night."

"That may be," Carlyle replied, "but if you only knew how I suffer waiting for him to crow!"

That's often our problem when we worry. We anticipate the negative so much that it destroys our peace and
minimizes our effectiveness. Montaigne, the philosopher,
said, "My life has been filled with terrible misfortune,
most of which never happened." Research has proven
that to be true for all of us. On the average,

- Forty percent of our worries never happen.
- Thirty percent are concerns of the past that we
  can't change anyway.
- Twelve percent are needless health worries.
- Ten percent are petty concerns.
- Only 8 percent of the things we worry about are
  really legitimate concerns.

I know of a woman who was terrified she would get
cancer. She talked about it frequently. She worried about
it constantly. She died in her late seventies of a heart attack! She spent her entire life worrying about the wrong
disease!

WORRY IS A SIN AGAINST GOD

The most important reason to conquer our habit of
worrying is that the Bible calls worry a sin. When we
worry, we directly violate God's commands. His Word
says, "Do not be anxious about anything" (Philippians
4:6) and, "Do not worry" (Matthew 6:25). Worry is a sin,
because when we worry we are refusing to put faith in
God. Worry calls God a liar.

- God promises, "I am with you always" (Matthew
  28:20). Worry insists, I'm all alone.
- God promises that "in all things God works for the
  good of those who love him" (Romans 8:28). Worry
  says, I don't think this will work out in my case.
- God promises that "I can do everything through
  him who gives me strength" (Philippians 4:13).
  Worry says, I can't do what God asks me to do.

One writer said that anxiety is the mark of spiritual insecurity. Another defined worry as "assuming responsibility that God never intended me to have." Only God has control of the future. To worry is to play God, trying to control what is beyond our ability to control. When we worry, we are refusing to put faith in God and we are breaking His command.

GOD'S PROMISES TO THOSE WHO WORRY

Despite our constant struggle with anxiety, God patiently waits for us to heed His promises to us in times of worry.

PRESENCE OF A COMPASSIONATE FRIEND

Cast all your anxiety on him because he cares for you.

1 Peter 5:7

As we have discussed in several previous chapters, one of God's promises we should always remember, whether we are worried, afraid, or feeling lonely, is that God is always with us. We have more than just His providential eye. He has given us His Holy Spirit—a constant companion, counselor, comforter, and friend.

"Do not let your hearts be troubled. Trust in God; trust also in me. . . . And I will ask the Father, and he will give you another Counselor to be with you forever—the Spirit of truth. . . . But the Counselor, the Holy Spirit, whom the Father will send in my name, will teach you all things and will remind you of everything I have said to you."

John 14:1, 16, 17, 26

We don't have to worry about facing the world alone or making wrong decisions or "doing something stupid," because God has promised us the great counselor to guide and comfort us.

PROVISIONS ONE DAY AT A TIME

Do you worry about things that *might* happen tomorrow or next week or way out in the future? There are thousands of things we could worry about.

- What if we run out of groceries before the next paycheck?
- What if I'm not prepared for retirement?
- What if my kids don't have enough money for college?
- What if my house burns down?
- What if I get fired?
- What if my child rebels?
- What if my spouse dies?

Remember God promises us only today's provisions. Jesus expects us to plan wisely for the future (see Luke 14:28-30), but He commands us not to worry about what hasn't happened. Only God knows the future, and most likely, He has not told you much about it. You must trust in Him to provide for you, one day at a time.

In chapter four I quoted from Matthew 6:25-34. Jesus' words in that passage are so applicable to us, not only in times of financial stress, but in any time of worry, that I want share the passage with you again. In the Sermon on the Mount, Jesus said:

"Therefore I tell you, do not worry about your life, what you will eat or drink; or about your body, what you will wear. Is not life more important than food, and the body more important than clothes? Look at the birds of the air; they do not sow or reap or store away in barns, and yet your heavenly Father feeds them. Are you not much more valuable than they? Who of you by worrying can add a single hour to his life?

"And why do you worry about clothes? See how the lilies of the field grow. They do not labor or spin. Yet I tell you that not even Solomon in all his splendor was dressed like one of

these. If that is how God clothes the grass of the field, which is here today and tomorrow is thrown into the fire, will he not much more clothe you, O you of little faith? So do not worry, saying, 'What shall we eat?' or 'What shall we drink?' or 'What shall we wear?' For the pagans run after all these things, and your heavenly Father knows that you need them. But seek first his kingdom and his righteousness, and all these things will be given to you as well. Therefore do not worry about tomorrow, for tomorrow will worry about itself. Each day has enough trouble of its own."

Matthew 6:25-34

What great advice! Those words were spoken nearly two thousand years ago, yet Jesus knew what we needed to hear. We chase after the same things the pagans chase after, and we teach our children to do the same. We worry about what we will eat. Will everyone like the dinner? Can we find a place to eat out that everyone likes? Can we be sure our groceries will last to the next paycheck?

We even worry about something as simple as what we will wear. Is this dress in style? Do my shirts have the right labels on them? Is my tie too wide or too narrow? Will the holes in my socks show?

Maybe your worries are more serious—you worry about your cancer recurring, your child's divorce, your financial stability—but worrying still doesn't change a thing. Jesus said, "Do you really think you will live one hour longer if you worry?" (see Matthew 6:27). We know that worrying actually shortens our life span, as we discussed earlier.

Jesus commands us to "just say no" to worry. According to Jesus, worry is a choice. To say "I just can't help worrying about this" is a cop-out. But most of us have made such excuses, which reveals how challenging it is to depend completely on God instead of our own efforts.

We don't like giving up control. We think if we worry enough we will be on guard; we'll be prepared; we won't be surprised; we might even have a chance to change the outcome of some terrible experience. Satan would like nothing better than for you to believe that you can control the future if you worry enough about it. That's just not true.

Trusting in God's daily provisions for our needs is a constant discipline. One woman told me, "I turn my problems over to the Lord and feel good. Then the next day I take them back!" You may decide to give up control of a part of your life, then realize later you have tried to wrestle control back from God.

An old song said, "Take your burden to the Lord and *leave it there!*" Here are five questions you can ask yourself to help take your focus off your worries and depend on God:

1. Have I prayed about this? The Bible commands us to pray about everything (Philippians 4:6). The hymn says,

> *O what peace we often forfeit,*
> *O what needless pain we bear,*
> *All because we do not carry*
> *Ev'rything to God in prayer!*

("What a Friend We Have In Jesus," Joseph M. Scriven.)

2. Do I believe what I say I believe? Martin Luther once went through a period of depression. After he had moped around the house for several days, his wife came down for breakfast one morning wearing all black. "Who died?" he asked.

"God did," she said.

"That's ridiculous!" Luther said.

"Well, then, why don't you act like it?" she asked.

Do you believe there is a God in Heaven who loves you as a father and will take care of your needs as He promised? Then act like it!

3. Can I survive the worst possible scenario with God's help? Instead of fearing the worst, face it. What is the worst thing that could possibly happen? Can you handle it with God's help? God has promised to be with you and strengthen you through the Holy Spirit so that you can face those times.

4. One hundred years from now, what will it matter? One hundred years from now, you will be with the Lord. The problems that seem gigantic now will appear so small then. Paul said, "I consider that our present sufferings are not worth comparing with the glory that will be revealed in us" (Romans 8:18).

5. Am I making the most of today? Since you cannot control the future, don't let worry rob you of the chance to live today to the fullest. "This is the day the Lord has made; let us rejoice and be glad in it" (Psalm 118:24).

PEACE THAT PASSES UNDERSTANDING

When we do make the decision to let God provide, He not only frees us from worry, He promises us the "peace that passes understanding" (see Philippians 4:7, KJV). If anyone had reason to worry, it was the apostle Paul, who wrote those words. As he sat in a Roman prison knowing his life was in grave danger, he wrote to his friends in Philippi about how he had learned to be content whatever the circumstances, saying, "I can do everything through him who gives me strength" (Philippians 4:13). He gave the Philippians this advice about worry:

Do not be anxious about anything, but in everything, by prayer and petition, with thanksgiving, present your requests to God. And the peace of God, which transcends all understanding, will guard your hearts and your minds in Christ Jesus.   *Philippians 4:6, 7*

In those verses, Paul gives a prescription for overcoming worry that is better than tranquilizers, alcohol, or sleeping pills. He says,

1. Make a choice that you are not going to worry. "Don't be anxious about anything."

2. "Pray about everything." Tell God about it. Do not try to control it on your own. Give your troubles to the only one who truly can do something about them.

Cast your cares on the Lord
and he will sustain you;
he will never let the righteous fall.   Psalm 55:22

3. Pray "with thanksgiving." There is nothing that changes your attitude like gratitude. We sing, "Count your many blessings, name them one by one, And it will surprise you what the Lord hath done." It is true. In fact, one stanza of that old hymn is particularly applicable:

Are you ever burdened with a load of care?
Does the cross seem heavy you are called to
bear?
Count your many blessings, every doubt will fly,
And you will be singing as the days go by.

("Count Your Blessings," Johnson Oatman, Jr.)

If you're ever having trouble falling asleep because you are worried, try to tell God all the things you're thankful for. If you can think of nothing, go through the alphabet. Begin with "A" and think of all the things starting with "A" that you are thankful for, no matter how big or small. "Lord, I'm thankful for America, angels watching over me, my favorite aunt, apple pie." Then go to the next letter. "God, I'm thankful for my beautiful bride, a soft bed, college basketball." You probably will never get to "Z" without falling asleep!

One teenage girl, who was going through a difficult time in her life, told me that when she had trouble falling asleep she would do a similar thing, praying for people she knew. She would go through the alphabet, praying for those with names beginning with "A," then "B," and so on. She usually would fall asleep about halfway through. She said she felt sorry for people whose names began with letters after "M" because she wasn't sure anyone ever prayed for them!

The Bible promises such physical rest as a result of the peace that comes to the person who trusts in Christ.

I will lie down and sleep in peace,
for you alone, O Lord,
make me dwell in safety. Psalm 4:8

He who dwells in the shelter of the Most High
will rest in the shadow of the Almighty.
I will say of the Lord, "He is my refuge and my
fortress,
my God, in whom I trust." Psalm 91:1, 2

When you lie down, you will not be afraid;
when you lie down, your sleep will be sweet.
Proverbs 3:24

But don't wait till insomnia drives you to pray with thanksgiving. It should be a daily discipline. Nothing will destroy anxiety like praising and thanking God each day. That is why the psalmist wrote:

Enter his gates with thanksgiving
and his courts with praise;
give thanks to him and praise his name." Psalm 100:4

Paul said if we will do three things—say no to worry, bring all our troubles to God, and pray with thanksgiving—then God will give us a peace that is beyond understanding.

Larry Burkett, a Christian author and financial counselor, went through a difficult time when he had his shoulder blade removed after a bout with cancer. But he reflected on what this world would be like if it weren't for Christ. He said, "If you aren't a Christian, this world is all the Heaven you will ever know. But if you are a Christian, this world is all the Hell you will ever know." When you realize how brief this life really is, and that we are headed toward a perfect eternity, you have no reason to worry.

[Jesus said,] "Peace I leave with you; my peace I give you. I do not give to you as the world gives. Do not let your hearts be troubled and do not be afraid."   *John 14:27*

Great peace have they who love your law,
  and nothing can make them stumble.   *Psalm 119:165*

You will keep in perfect peace
  him whose mind is steadfast,
  because he trusts in you.   *Isaiah 26:3*

IN TIMES OF OPPOSITION

Acts 16:11-40

Johnny Hart, the creator of "B.C." and "The Wizard of Id," has been drawing comic strips for thirty-six years. He has been recognized six times by the National Cartoonist Society for Best Humor Strip of the Year. His columns appear regularly in nearly every major newspaper across the country. But *The Los Angeles Times* refused to run Hart's "B.C." cartoon on Palm Sunday in 1996. The reason? The editors told Hart, who is a Christian, that he was being censored for the day because the message of the cartoon he submitted was too "religious" (*World* magazine, April 20, 1996, pp. 12-15).

Columnist Cal Thomas was once bumped from "Good Morning, America" when he was scheduled to do an interview about homosexuality in San Francisco. The producer explained, "My senior producer was afraid you would get on and quote some Bible verses."

"You'll have every other screwball on that show," Thomas protested. "They even mention God in a blasphemous way on some of your entertainment programs. Are you saying I can't speak well of Him?" But Cal Thomas was excluded. He says he has come to expect that kind of treatment from members of the major media (Ibid., pp. 12-15).

Supreme Court Justice Antonin Scalia spoke about his personal faith at a prayer breakfast in Jackson, Mississippi, urging the 650 people who were present to ignore the scorn of the "worldly wise" and stand up for their beliefs. Immediately, members of the national media began to protest Scalia's public expression of faith. One cartoonist attempted to lampoon Justice Scalia by showing him reading a Bible while his fellow justices read the Constitution.

We shouldn't be surprised or discouraged when Christians in prominent positions are scorned by their peers. Jesus warned that we would face opposition. He said:

"Remember the words I spoke to you: 'No servant is greater than his master.' If they persecuted me, they will persecute you also. If they obeyed my teaching, they will obey yours also."   John 15:20

Even though opposition in America is increasing, we know little of the intense persecution believers face in other countries. Christians in predominantly Muslim countries, for example, often encounter intense opposition from those in the majority religion. Robert Hussein, a Kuwaiti convert to Christianity, went on trial in civil court in Kuwait City on April 17, 1996, for apostasy (abandonment of Islam). He knew that if he was convicted, he faced the forced dissolution of his marriage and the loss of certain civil rights, including the right to see his children. He feared that some Muslims would interpret a guilty ruling as permission to kill him, because there is likely to be no punishment for killing an apostate of Islam in his country. Hussein was found guilty but was able to flee to the United States. In America, though he may face an occasional critic, he is free to worship as he chooses without fear of punishment.

PAUL AND SILAS FACED OPPOSITION

Paul and Silas healed a slave girl of her demon posses-
sion. But the slave's owners, instead of being happy for
her, were angry with the two missionaries. The girl's
demon had given her psychic powers, and her ability to
tell the future had made the owners rich. When their
source of income was eliminated, they were enraged.
They probably told everyone that the girl had a "gift"
which allowed her to tell the future, and that Paul and
Silas had "messed with her mind." It was really the other
way around. The demon had messed with her mind. Paul
and Silas had given her a clear mind, and the greatest gift
of all, Jesus Christ.

The slave owners dragged Paul and Silas before the authorities. They said, "These men are Jews, and are throw-
ing our city into an uproar by advocating customs
unlawful for us Romans to accept or practice" (Acts 16:20,
21). The criticism wasn't true, but a mob had formed.
The city rulers, seeking peace instead of justice, flogged
Paul and Silas and threw them in jail.

How would you react in the face of such opposition? I
know what I would be tempted to do—gripe, grow bitter,
give in, and promise never to preach again in that city so
I could save my own skin. But the leaders of the early
church were made of a different stock than most of us
today.

*About midnight Paul and Silas were praying and singing
hymns to God, and the other prisoners were listening to them.*
Acts 16:25

If nothing else were written about the event, that verse
alone would inspire us. Later, when Paul wrote to his
friends in that city of Philippi, he said, "Rejoice in the
Lord always. I will say it again: Rejoice!" (Philippians 4:4).
They knew he practiced what he preached! Paul had

found a way to praise the Lord in the midst of terrible circumstances.

God rewarded the courage of Paul and Silas.

Suddenly there was such a violent earthquake that the foundations of the prison were shaken. At once all the prison doors flew open, and everybody's chains came loose. The jailer woke up, and when he saw the prison doors open, he drew his sword and was about to kill himself because he thought the prisoners had escaped." Acts 16:26, 27

The jailer must have feared that the city rulers would execute him for letting the prisoners escape, even though he couldn't have prevented the earthquake. He drew his sword to kill himself.

But Paul shouted, "Don't harm yourself! We are all here! Acts 16:28

Paul and Silas cared more about the jailer than they did their own freedom. The jailer was stunned that those who had been persecuted would treat him with such kindness. He knew he was in the presence of godly men. His heart was open, and he asked what he had to do to be saved from his evil deeds. Paul and Silas led him to Christ on the spot!

At that hour of the night the jailer took them and washed their wounds; then immediately he and all his family were baptized. Acts 16:33

What courage they showed in the face of opposition! Paul and Silas knew the Lord could save them, but even if He chose not to, they were determined to praise Him. They counted themselves worthy to suffer for Christ. Paul later wrote to his friends in Philippi:

For it has been granted to you on behalf of Christ not only to

believe on him, but also to suffer for him, since you are going
through the same struggle you saw I had, and now hear that I
still have.   Philippians 1:29, 30

PROMISES IN OPPOSITION

"It has been *granted* to you . . . to *suffer* for him," Paul
said. Paul and Silas saw it as a privilege to be persecuted
in the name of Christ. They knew God would take care
of them in His time, because He had promised to do so.
When we face opposition, we can also take comfort in
God's promises.

YOU WILL RECEIVE OPPOSITION

In earlier chapters I've discussed this truth in a different light. Just as God promises that you will be tempted
and you will face trials, God promises that if you are following Him, you will be opposed. Jesus said, "All men
will hate you because of me" (Luke 21:17).

Paul warned Timothy, "In fact, everyone who wants to
live a godly life in Christ Jesus will be persecuted" (2
Timothy 3:12). In our nation we may not experience the
physical persecution like the early Christians did, but
God promises that if we follow Him we will face opposition. We will be criticized, confronted, opposed, and de-
serted.

I am privileged to be a part of a church that has been
blessed by God. We have witnessed thousands of people
come to Christ. But the larger our church grows, the
more criticism we encounter. A few years ago a member
of our church was arrested for murder. He had only been
attending our church for three months, and he had committed the crime more than a year earlier. But a local television station filmed a news clip in front of our church,
showing his picture and claiming that he was active in our

congregation. They didn't say where he worked, how long he had lived in Louisville, or any other personal information, yet they found it necessary to report his involvement in our church. They didn't even explain how short a time he had been attending. False rumors began to circulate that the man had been a leader in our congregation!

On another occasion, our local paper wrote a very nice article about our church. Then a few weeks later someone wrote a letter to the editor, slamming our church for being "bigheaded" and always "striving to be the biggest and the best." The letter claimed we should have started more churches so we wouldn't have grown so large. The writer obviously didn't know how many churches we have helped get off the ground or have helped financially through difficult times over the years.

I was once complaining to my friend Steve Chapman about someone's criticism of me when Steve said, "Well, at least you got that 'woe' off your back."

I said, "What are you talking about?"

He said, "Jesus said, 'Woe to you when all men speak well of you.' Obviously, all men are not speaking well of you, so that's one 'woe' you don't have to worry about!"

Steve Chapman was right. Jesus said if you're getting along with everyone, something is wrong (see Luke 6:26). We will encounter opposition when we do the Lord's will.

GOD WILL HELP YOU RESPOND TO OPPOSITION

"This [persecution] will result in your being witnesses to them. But make up your mind not to worry beforehand how you will defend yourselves. For I will give you words and wisdom that none of your adversaries will be able to resist or contradict."   Luke 21:13-15

When we face opposition, the Holy Spirit will be there to tell us what to say. What a promise! Jesus said to His disciples:

"But when they arrest you, do not worry about what to say or how to say it. At that time you will be given what to say, for it will not be you speaking, but the Spirit of your Father speaking through you."   Matthew 10:19, 20

I was once asked to speak about Christianity to a college class studying world religions. After my speech, a boy raised his hand and asked, "How can you base your belief on the Gospels when they contradict themselves?"

I wanted to ask, "What contradictions do you have in mind?" Most of the time when people ask that question, they're just repeating what they have heard others say. They really don't know of any specific examples of the Bible contradicting itself, because such supposed contradictions are rare and are usually explained through understanding the context and customs of the day. But I didn't ask him that question, because I didn't want to embarrass the young man in front of his peers. (I was also afraid he might have a contradiction for which I didn't have a good explanation!) Instead, I asked, "If you were a judge in a courtroom and four eyewitnesses to a crime gave verbatim testimonies, what would you conclude?"

"That they were all lying," he answered.

"Why?" I pressed.

"Because they obviously corroborated their story, or they wouldn't be able to give the exact same testimony," he said.

"Right," I said. "The Gospels are not verbatim, because each witness comes from a different angle. The Bible doesn't read like a lie."

That was one time I felt like the Holy Spirit had really helped me respond to opposition! There are certainly times when we don't respond like we want, and we look back wishing we had said something else. Yet I think there are many times when we may not even realize it, but the Holy Spirit is guiding us to say just what He wants us to say in the face of opposition.

Dealing with criticism and confrontation is probably the closest most of us will get to facing persecution. Therefore, let me share some reminders about handling criticism, so that we can keep our personal desires out of the way and let God speak through us whenever we are opposed.

1. Remember that all leaders are criticized. If you carry the ball, you are going to get tackled. If you are a leader, you will receive criticism. Negative notes and phone calls, petty comments, and anonymous letters are inevitable. The larger our church grows, the more criticism I receive. I occasionally look out into the congregation and see the skeptical local leaders of a certain religious denomination sitting in the back pews. While I am preaching, they fold their arms and scowl at me. When I say something with which they disagree, they lean over and mumble to one another. They don't make it easy to preach! But their opposition should be a reminder to me that God is using our church in a powerful way. We are being criticized because we are "carrying the ball."

2. Evaluate the source. An outspoken church member in a rural congregation walked by the new preacher after church one Sunday morning and said, "Preacher, that's the worst sermon I have ever heard in my life!"

The new preacher was really disturbed until an elder put a reassuring arm around his shoulder and said, "Don't pay any attention to him, son. He's not quite right upstairs. He just goes around repeating what he hears other people saying."

Ask yourself, "Is it a petty, small-minded person who is griping, or someone whom I respect?" When criticism comes from someone who is a constant complainer, ignore it and go on.

3. Weigh the objection. The criticism might be valid. If so, then thank the person for his concern and make the necessary adjustment. If it is based on untruth, ignore it. Truth has a way of surfacing in time. When you answer an untrue criticism, you usually give it more validity than it merits.

4. Keep your focus. Don't grumble about the critics. Do not let Satan distract you from your primary purpose. Your assignment is to please Christ, not men. His is the only opinion that really matters. People are fickle. The same people who criticize you today may be singing your praises tomorrow.

5. Maintain a sense of humor. Sometimes there is nothing you can do about petty criticisms but laugh. A skeptical reporter once saw Billy Graham disembark the Queen Mary and quipped, "When Jesus was on earth, He rode a lowly donkey. I can't imagine Jesus arriving from England on a luxury ocean liner."
Grady Wilson, one of Graham's associates, laughed. "Find me a donkey that can swim the Atlantic and I'll buy it!" he said.

6. Give God thanks. Thank God that you were counted worthy to carry the ball and to receive opposition because of your faithfulness. When you can begin to receive criticism with thanks and praise to God, then you'll know you are growing in faith and love.

GOD WILL BLESS YOU FOR ENDURING OPPOSITION
[Jesus said,] "Blessed are those who are persecuted because of righteousness, for theirs is the kingdom of heaven.

"Blessed are you when people insult you, persecute you and falsely say all kinds of evil against you because of me. Rejoice and be glad, because great is your reward in heaven, for in the

same way they persecuted the prophets who were before you."
Matthew 5:10-12

The Living Bible paraphrases the word "blessed" as
"happy." You will be happy when you experience persecution. It's hard to imagine how that could be true, but it
is. There are two reasons:

1. Your faith is strengthened. Those who have en-
dured persecution for Christ's sake have testified to the
blessings they have received following their experiences.
They seem to wear their persecutions as badges of
courage, proud that they were able to suffer in the name
of Christ. Johnny Hart said that his treatment by *The Los
Angeles Times* is symptomatic of the battle for America's
soul. He says he likes "the idea that this has gotten Christians up in arms" *(World* magazine, April 20, 1996, p. 12).

Paul said a similar thing about his experiences in
prison: "Because of my chains, most of the brothers in
the Lord have been encouraged to speak the word of
God more courageously and fearlessly" (Philippians 1:14).

2. Your church is purified. The story is often told
that when Russia was still under communist rule, during
a time when Christians were being persecuted, two Russ-
ian soldiers barged in on a small congregation meeting in
someone's basement. They lined up the thirty members
of the church against the walls and said, "Leave now and
renounce Christ, or stay and be executed." A few left, but
most stayed. When the doors were closed, the soldiers
put down their guns. "We are Christians, too," the soldiers said. "But we dare not worship with anyone who is
not authentic. May we worship with you?"

Only those who are committed to Christ will with-
stand persecution. When your church endures a period
of opposition, those who are not strong will fall away.
But you will witness a new sense of unity and fellowship

among those who remain. People will be happy that the church has been purified.

Facing opposition is not fun, but when we encounter criticism or persecution, we can "rejoice that we participate in the sufferings of Christ." God has promised that such opposition will be part of the Christian life. But don't be afraid. He has promised to be with you, to give you the words to say, and He promises to bless you eternally if you persevere.

The Lord is my light and my salvation—
* whom shall I fear?*
The Lord is the stronghold of my life—
* of whom shall I be afraid?*
When evil men advance against me to devour my flesh,
when my enemies and my foes attack me,
* they will stumble and fall.*
Though an army besiege me,
* my heart will not fear;*
though war break out against me,
* even then will I be confident. . . .*

Do not turn me over to the desire of my foes,
* for false witnesses rise up against me,*
* breathing out violence.*

I am still confident of this:
* I will see the goodness of the Lord*
* in the land of the living.*
Wait for the Lord;
* be strong and take heart*
* and wait for the Lord.*   *Psalm 27:1-3, 12-14*

IN TIMES OF PROSPERITY

Genesis 41:41-57

In a book about God's promises for troubled times, it probably seems strange that I would include a chapter on prosperity. Yet more people struggle with their faith during prosperous times than during times of adversity. I have heard it said that for every one man who can stand prosperity, there are a hundred that will stand adversity. Difficult times tend to draw us close to God and make us depend on Him. But when things are going well, we are tempted to forget God and do things our own way.

The first three kings of Israel proved that to be true. All three handled adversity well but fell away from God during times of prosperity.

- King Saul was so self-conscious when he was first anointed king that he hid from the crowd, but after a few years of success he became so arrogant that he attempted to kill his successor.
- King David was so pure when he was a young man that he was described as a man after God's own heart (1 Samuel 13:14), but after his success and power as king he committed adultery and murder.
- King Solomon began his political career by humbly

122

praying, "Who am I to govern so great a people? Lord, grant me wisdom" (1 Kings 3:6-10, paraphrased). God gave him both wisdom and wealth. But in his time of prosperity, Solomon became depressed and foolish, indulging himself in every way and eventually marrying seven hundred wives.

We could name dozens of famous people in recent history who made it through terrible times of adversity but fell apart when life seemed to be going so well for them. Elvis Presley, Jimmy Bakker, Richard Nixon, Karen Carpenter, and many others reached the pinnacle of success against great odds but failed to handle the trials that came from their success. *Fortune* magazine, in an article titled "The Trophy Wife Is Back With Brains," revealed that many businessmen who achieve financial success are tempted to leave their wives and marry younger women, thinking they deserve some reward for their accomplishments. "'Powerful men are beginning to demand trophy wives. The culture of self-indulgence has just crept up to the CEO level,' says Boston psychologist Harry Levinson, a longtime counselor of top management. 'Indulgence is an issue for people who have worked very hard to get where they are. They feel they've earned it . . . they're entitled to it'" *(Fortune,* April 3, 1995, p. 102).

One preacher said, "Not every man can carry a full cup." Few people can maintain their spiritual equilibrium when they have reached the pinnacle of success.

C. S. Lewis said, "Prosperity is good campaigning weather for the Devil."

JOSEPH'S PROSPERITY

While it appears that most do not handle prosperity well, there are few biblical examples of people who maintained their integrity in times of tremendous success. One of those few was Joseph.

Everyone marvels at the integrity of Joseph through his times of *adversity* in his early adult years. He didn't renounce his faith or become bitter when his brothers sold him to slave traders. He kept his purity when he was a young slave in Egypt and his master's wife tried to seduce him. When the rejected woman accused him of trying to rape her and he was thrown into prison, he still held on to his faith in God (see Genesis 37-39).

What is even more rare, however, is the way Joseph dealt with the instant *prosperity* that came to him literally overnight. After many years as a slave and two long years in prison, he suddenly found himself at the pinnacle of success.

Joseph had become known in prison for his ability to interpret dreams. When Pharaoh had a terrible nightmare, the cupbearer suddenly remembered the time he was in prison and a young man interpreted his dream. As soon as the cupbearer told Pharaoh, he demanded that Joseph be brought to him.

So Pharaoh sent for Joseph, and he was quickly brought from the dungeon. When he had shaved and changed his clothes, he came before Pharaoh.

Pharaoh said to Joseph, "I had a dream, and no one can interpret it. But I have heard it said of you that when you hear a dream you can interpret it."

"I cannot do it," Joseph replied to Pharaoh, "but God will give Pharaoh the answer he desires."   Genesis 41:14-16

Pharaoh described a dream in which seven fat cows came out of the Nile River, then seven thin cows came and devoured the seven fat cows. Then he saw seven good heads of grain grow on a single stalk, followed by seven withered heads that swallowed up the seven good heads.

Joseph told Pharaoh that the dream was from God. A

time of prosperity was coming, when Egypt would enjoy seven good years of crops. Then a time of famine would come—a long drought lasting seven years. The drought would be so bad that the people would forget about the seven years of prosperity.

Joseph then gave this wise advice to Pharaoh:

"And now let Pharaoh look for a discerning and wise man and put him in charge of the land of Egypt. Let Pharaoh appoint commissioners over the land to take a fifth of the harvest of Egypt during the seven years of abundance. They should collect all the food of these good years that are coming and store up the grain under the authority of Pharaoh, to be kept in the cities for food. This food should be held in reserve for the country, to be used during the seven years of famine that will come upon Egypt, so that the country may not be ruined by the famine." Genesis 41:33-36

Pharaoh decided there couldn't be a wiser man than Joseph, so he placed the young Israelite slave in charge of the collection and distribution of the nation's reserves. In one day Joseph went from a dungeon cell to second in command to the pharaoh himself in the most powerful nation in the world. Joseph had been poor, lonely, and enslaved in a dungeon. Suddenly he was rich, famous, and powerful.

Such accounts of success in the Bible are usually accompanied by stories of pride, misused power, misplaced priorities, and a loss of integrity. But Joseph maintained his integrity and continued to be obedient to God through the next fourteen years of service in Egypt. The time of prosperity brought added temptations for Joseph, but with the help of God he handled them all well. He suddenly had the power to take revenge against those who had hurt him—Potiphar's wife, the cupbearer who forgot him, his wicked brothers—yet he chose to forgive.

He could have had any woman he wanted, but he chose to remain faithful to his wife. He could have become lazy, but he chose to keep working hard. He could have taken the credit himself for his success, but he chose to give glory to God.

GOD'S PROMISES IN PROSPERITY

The story of Joseph reveals several promises God makes to His people that we should remember in times of prosperity.

GOD GRANTS PROSPERITY TO THE RIGHTEOUS

[The righteous man] is like a tree planted by
  streams of water,
  which yields its fruit in season
and whose leaf does not wither.
  Whatever he does prospers.   *Psalm 1:3*

God has promised a certain amount of prosperity to those who are righteous. That doesn't mean that you will never face adversity or that your prosperity will match Joseph's, or even that you will always be prosperous. However, you will experience a certain amount of success in this life if you follow God.

[David said to Solomon,] "Then you will have success if you are careful to observe the decrees and laws that the Lord gave Moses for Israel."   *1 Chronicles 22:13*

[Uzziah] sought God during the days of Zechariah, who instructed him in the fear of God. As long as he sought the Lord, God gave him success.   *2 Chronicles 26:5*

In everything that [Hezekiah] undertook in the service of God's temple and in obedience to the law and the commands, he sought his God and worked wholeheartedly. And so he prospered.   *2 Chronicles 31:21*

The first step in handling prosperity correctly is acknowledging that your success is a gift from God and not a result of your own abilities. There are three recorded instances where Joseph acknowledged that his rise to prominence was a gift from God.

1. Joseph gave credit to God for his ability to interpret dreams. When Pharaoh said that he had heard Joseph could interpret dreams, Joseph corrected him. "'I cannot do it,' Joseph replied to Pharaoh, 'but God will give Pharaoh the answer he desires'" (Genesis 41:16).

2. Joseph gave thanks to God for his children. Joseph was blessed by God with not only riches and power but a beautiful wife and two healthy sons. To show his gratitude to God, he named the first son Manasseh, which sounds like the Hebrew word for "forget," saying, "It is because God has made me forget all my trouble" (Genesis 41:51). He named his second son Ephraim, which means "twice fruitful," saying, "It is because God has made me fruitful in the land of my suffering" (Genesis 41:52).

3. Joseph gave honor to God for working all things together for good. Years later, during the seven years of famine, Joseph's brothers suddenly appeared in Egypt looking for food to take back to their families in Canaan. They didn't recognize Joseph. It had been more than two decades since they had seen him. He was twenty years older, and he dressed and spoke like an Egyptian. Joseph had the perfect opportunity to exact revenge against his brothers. He could have had them tortured or executed, and no one would have questioned him. But Joseph knew that God had used their evil deeds for His good will, and Joseph needed to forgive them. In a dramatic moment, Joseph revealed himself to his brothers.

Joseph said to his brothers, "I am Joseph! Is my father still living?" But his brothers were not able to answer him, because they were terrified at his presence.

Then Joseph said to his brothers, "Come close to me." When they had done so, he said, "I am your brother Joseph, the one you sold into Egypt! And now, do not be distressed and do not be angry with yourselves for selling me here, because it was to save lives that God sent me ahead of you. For two years now there has been famine in the land, and for the next five years there will not be plowing and reaping. But God sent me ahead of you to preserve for you a remnant on earth and to save your lives by a great deliverance.

"So then, it was not you who sent me here, but God."

Genesis 45:3-8

THE PROSPEROUS WILL FACE TEMPTATIONS

The Bible promises that temptations will intensify if you are successful. Prosperity always threatens our spirituality in several ways.

Pride. It's tempting for those who achieve status and wealth to believe they are truly superior to those beneath them. *In Rebuilding Your Broken World,* Gordon MacDonald noted that "few things kill the soul faster than becoming addicted to the applause of people." He cautioned readers to accept praise with graciousness and then "renounce it in the heart lest it lodge there and become believable."

"Pride goes before destruction, a haughty spirit before a fall."

Proverbs 16:18

Greed. You would think that the more a person accumulates, the more generous he would become. But materialism is such a cancer that we lose perspective about what is important. We always feel like we'd like to have just a little more.

Indulgence. In 1950 Americans spent 10 percent of their income on luxuries. By 1980 we were spending 30 percent on luxuries. Jesus told of a rich man who lived in the lap of luxury but ignored the poor man searching through his garbage each night for food (Luke 16).

Jimmy Bakker, the television evangelist, took money from people who were living on Social Security and paid himself hundreds of thousands of dollars in bonuses. When you prosper, it's easy to get in the habit of indulging in nice vacations, top-of-the-line restaurants, luxury cars, and expensive hobbies, while never giving anything to assist the needy around you.

Laziness. The higher we climb, the more likely we are to have people serving under us, doing the work for us. It becomes easy to delegate responsibility and assume that everything will go along fine while we eat, drink, and are merry. King David was a mighty warrior, but in the middle of his life he began to think he was too valuable to his kingdom to go to war. He stayed home and rested while his underlings did the fighting. It was during a time when his troops were at war but he was at home, lounging on his balcony, that he fell into lust and adultery with his next-door neighbor, Bathsheba.

False security. Instead of putting our trust in God, we can subconsciously trust in our accumulation of stocks, savings and life insurance policies. Jesus told about a farmer who prospered tremendously during one harvest season. But instead of thanking God and being generous with what he had, the man planned to build bigger barns and hoard his wealth. He was preparing an insurance policy for himself. He thought by storing it up, he would be secure and be able to eat, drink, and be merry for many years to come. But God came to him and said, "You fool! This very night your life will be demanded from you. Then who will get what you have prepared for yourself?" (Luke 12:20).

Distraction. This is perhaps the most dangerous pitfall, because it is so subtle. Success brings added responsibility. When things start going well, you can get so busy maintaining the new responsibilities that there is no time for spiritual things. You never meant for that to happen; in your mind you're still the same dedicated Christian you once were. But your lifestyle has become so hectic that you just can't seem to afford the time to go to church on Sundays, read your Bible every day, or spend regular time in prayer. You might even resign from your church responsibilities because you know you will be gone a lot, traveling on the weekends or working overtime.

J. C. Penney, one of the wealthiest men of his generation, said, "If a man is too busy to go to church twice on Sunday and once during the week, he has more business than God intended him to have." But it is a rare person who is able to succeed by the world's standards and still maintain his priorities. When you are on top, you face sleepless nights, unsolvable problems, and jealous people who put pressure on you. You feel so tired that you don't fellowship with Christian friends like you once did. You find yourself running with the jet set. They have habits that aren't consistent with your values, but you don't want to seem naive, so you go along.

You keep saying, "We've got to slow down. We've got to get back into church and family values. As soon as we get through this season, we're going to do it." But often those who say such things never do. It doesn't get any better. One day you realize Satan has so distracted you in your prosperity that you are a shell of the person you once were.

YOU CAN HANDLE PROSPERITY WITH GOD'S HELP

With all these dangers, it is easy to feel like there is no way a successful person could get to Heaven. You can see why Jesus said, "I tell you the truth, it is hard for a rich man to enter the kingdom of heaven. Again I tell you, it is easier for a camel to go through the eye of a needle than for a rich man to enter the kingdom of God" (Matthew 19:23, 24).

You can also see why the disciples were "greatly astonished" and responded, "Who then can be saved?" (Matthew 19:25). If it is impossible for a rich man to enter Heaven, then why does God give riches to anyone? And if you were born in America, you are rich compared to the rest of the world. How then can anyone be saved?

Jesus looked at them and said, "With man this is impossible, but with God all things are possible."   Matthew 19:26

It's that simple. God created the camel. If He wants to put a camel through the eye of a needle, He can do it, but it would take His supernatural power. God can also overcome the barriers that keep a prosperous man from heaven. But only with God's supernatural help can you make it through prosperity and maintain your spiritual equilibrium.

Notice what Joseph did right with the help of God to maintain a proper spiritual perspective in a time of prosperity.

Joseph accepted the appointment willingly. Joseph knew that God was bringing him to prominence for a reason. He didn't express false humility and say, "Oh, shucks, I can't do that. I'm not really qualified to run this nation." Humility is not insecurity. Humility is finding out what God has gifted you to do and doing it for His glory instead of your own. Joseph accepted the position and went to work, knowing God would use him in his place of prominence.

Joseph was diligent for a prolonged period. Ten years later, well into the period of famine, the Bible still describes Joseph's involvement in leadership. He didn't quit, even though there were probably people who were critical of the way he collected or distributed the food.

He didn't give up even though it certainly got boring and routine at times. He worked hard, even though he probably could have retired and found someone else to do it for him.

Successful people know that the joy comes in the journey. When you reach the top and there is not much of a challenge left, you are tempted to get lazy and you begin to lose your self-esteem. The joy of the journey is gone. Life becomes boring and routine while you try to maintain your status as the top dog. It's difficult to be diligent in your work. You can begin to look for other challenges, sometimes turning to immoral things for fulfillment.

Joseph continued to work hard even though the challenge of getting to the top was no longer his to enjoy. He realized that true fulfillment can only come from doing what you know God has called you to do, even if it is routine or unchallenging at times. The Lord will bring additional challenges in His time.

Joseph remained faithful to his wife. Almost all the other Old Testament characters turned to polygamy or adultery when they reached the top of success. Like the businessmen mentioned earlier, they somehow thought their success gave them a right to chase after other indulgences.

One of the greatest temptations a successful man will face is the allure of other women who are attracted to him because of his success. But Proverbs 5:15, in a warning against adultery, says, "Drink water from your own cistern, running water from your own well." If you are a married man, your wife is not a trophy; she is a treasure. She is a valuable vessel and an heir with you of the promised gift of life. If you are not mature enough to express love to her and deepen in your companionship with her, then your ego is way out of control. Pray that God will restore in you a compassion for your wife and a renewed romance in your marriage.

I heard a preacher say, "If you are forty-five years old and are still turned on by an eighteen-year-old flighty teenager, there is something wrong with you. When we mature, what we find attractive in the opposite sex ought to mature also, things like poise, depth of character, and personality." The preacher said he knew he was getting older when he went to weddings and the mother of the bride was more attractive to him than the bride! I knew what he meant. I watched a rerun of "Leave It to Beaver" the other day, and Mrs. Cleaver looked good to me. I guess when I start watching "The Beverly Hillbillies" because Granny is looking good, it's time for the Lord to take me!

Don't live in an unrealistic fantasy world. Be content with the mate God has given you. Drink water from your own cistern.

Joseph used his position to benefit others. At first, Joseph thought he was being used by God to make sure the Egyptians stayed alive through the famine. He didn't realize until later the depth to which God was really using him—to save his own people from starvation and to carry on the remnant of the Jewish nation so that the Messiah might someday be born. But Joseph did what he could to benefit others, without thought of personal reward. And God used his willing heart.

A generous man will prosper;
*   he who refreshes others will himself be refreshed.*
                                        Proverbs 11:25

GOD WILL USE YOUR SUCCESS FOR HIS GLORY

Joseph soon realized that God had placed him in a prominent position at just the right time, for a special purpose. He told his brothers, "Do not be angry with yourselves for selling me here, because it was to save lives that God sent me ahead of you . . . God sent me . . . to preserve for you a remnant on earth and to save your lives by a great deliverance" (Genesis 45:5-7). Had it not been for Joseph's leadership, the Jewish nation might not have survived the famine.

When God chooses to give you a certain amount of prosperity or success, recognize that He has done so to reveal His glory or to accomplish His purpose. Watch for Him to reveal to you what that purpose might be. Even if you are unable to see it in this life, God has you where you are for a purpose. Maybe in time you'll be able to look back and see what that purpose was. In the meantime, recognize that your success comes from God, and look for opportunities to use your success for God's glory.

As I write this book, University of Florida quarterback Danny Wuerffel is a leading candidate for the 1996 Heisman trophy. Following the 1995 football season, he was invited to be a *Playboy* magazine All-American. The award included a vacation at an Arizona resort and a *Playboy* photo shoot. Wuerffel turned down the offer because of his Christian convictions. "It would have been a lot of fun, and that's fine for some," said Wuerffel, the son of an Air Force chaplain. "I'm sure there's a good bit of the population out there that would think I'm silly for doing this. But there's also a good bit of the population that would understand. That's not the kind of person I would want to portray myself as" ("Backfield Emotions," Dave Roos, *Courier Journal,* May 10, 1996). With his success has come both opportunity and temptation, but we can rejoice that Danny Wuerffel seems to be handling himself much like Joseph did. Because of his ability to play football, he has been given a platform from which to speak about Jesus Christ, and he has used that platform for God's glory.

God has not put you in a position of prominence that you might accumulate things and indulge yourself. You are there to be a positive influence for Christ. If you make money, share it wisely with those in need. If you are in a position of power, make decisions that are wise and sympathetic toward people. If you have become famous, use your fame to spread the gospel of Christ.

Times of prosperity are challenging times. Only by the power of God can you maintain your spiritual equilibrium. But God promises to give you the strength to make it through, and to use both your successes and your failures for His glory, if you will let Him.

"Do not let this Book of the Law depart from your mouth; meditate on it day and night, so that you may be careful to do everything written in it. Then you will be prosperous and successful."   *Joshua 1:8*

IN TIMES OF GRIEF

Job 1–42

As a minister I have conducted hundreds of funerals and witnessed thousands of people grieving over the loss of a loved one. It is especially difficult to conduct a service for a child who has passed away. Parents never consider that their children might precede them in death. I suppose few things in life could be as painful as losing a son or daughter, especially while he or she is still young.

I once conducted a funeral for a three-year-old girl who had been killed in an accident. As you can imagine, the funeral was a sad occasion. Her parents loved her so much. At the end of the service, after everyone had been dismissed except the parents, they stood at the casket while the organist—at their request—played the girl's favorite song: "You are my sunshine, my only sunshine. Please don't take my sunshine away." It was almost more than I could bear.

Though the loss of a loved one is probably the most common and painful type of grief, we mourn for many different reasons. Since there is one character in the Old Testament who experienced just about all of those reasons for grief, let's study the life of Job before discussing the promises of God in times of grief.

JOB'S REASONS TO GRIEVE

Perhaps no one in history had more reason to mourn than Job did. He experienced a series of tragic losses that could only be brought by the devil himself. God gave Satan permission to test Job for a time so that Satan could see how faithful Job was to God.

HE LOST ALL HIS WEALTH

Job had been a very rich man. He owned 7,000 sheep, 3,000 camels, 500 yoke of oxen and 500 donkeys (see Job 1:3). In today's market, someone estimated that Job's livestock would be worth about six million dollars! He also had scores of employees watching over his investments for him. He had it made. Yet in one day he lost it all.

One day when Job's sons and daughters were feasting and drinking wine at the oldest brother's house, a messenger came to Job and said, "The oxen were plowing and the donkeys were grazing nearby, and the Sabeans attacked and carried them off. They put the servants to the sword, and I am the only one who has escaped to tell you!"

While he was still speaking, another messenger came and said, "The fire of God fell from the sky and burned up the sheep and the servants, and I am the only one who has escaped to tell you!"

While he was still speaking, another messenger came and said, "The Chaldeans formed three raiding parties and swept down on your camels and carried them off. They put the servants to the sword, and I am the only one who has escaped to tell you!" Job 1:13-17

Violent crime and a natural disaster had robbed Job of everything. Job had no insurance policy to replace his belongings. There was no possibility of a lawsuit. He had no safety deposit box hidden somewhere or a retirement plan on which to rely. In one day, Job went from the penthouse to the poorhouse. He lost all his wealth and all of his employees who had faithfully worked for him.

On May 27, 1996, a tornado came ripping through Bullitt County, Kentucky, just a few minutes from our home in Louisville, damaging more than one thousand homes. One of the secretaries at our church, Dorleen Garrett, and her husband, Gene, lost nearly everything they owned. Gene saw the garbage being whipped around by the wind and went outside to gather it up, when suddenly the tornado hit. He had no time to get back inside, so he grabbed the front tire of his car. Just about the time he felt the car lifting off the ground, a tree came smashing down and pinned the car against the drive. Gene escaped with only a few abrasions, thankful to God that his life was spared.

Meanwhile, Dorleen, on the inside, heard the horrible sound of the tornado coming and ran for an inner wall. She said the storm lasted only one or two minutes, but it seemed like forever. "I was not just praying, I was shouting, hoping the Lord would hear me over all the crashing of glass and lumber." When the tornado had passed, the two met in the front yard of their ravaged home and embraced, so thankful that though they had lost nearly all of their material possessions, they were still alive and had each other.

HE LOST ALL HIS CHILDREN

Job had seven sons and three daughters. He loved them and was constantly praying for them. Yet in the same day that he lost all his possessions, the greatest tragedy he could imagine happened.

While [the messenger] was still speaking, yet another messenger came and said, "Your sons and daughters were feasting

and drinking wine at the oldest brother's house, when sud-
denly a mighty wind swept in from the desert and struck the
four corners of the house. It collapsed on them and they are
dead, and I am the only one who has escaped to tell you!"
Job 1:18, 19

Evidently a tornado struck the home of Job's oldest
son and killed everyone inside. We think it's tragic when
we hear on the news that a parent has lost one or even
two children in an accident. Can you imagine losing all
ten of your children at once?

To make it more difficult, their deaths were sudden.
Though we hate to see anyone suffer, when someone dies
slowly there is an opportunity to express your love, say
good-bye, and begin to prepare for life without the one
you love. If the death is unexpected, like an accident or a
heart attack, you feel cheated. There were things you did-
n't get to say. Sometimes there is guilt. Maybe your last
words were argumentative, or you wish you had done
something to prevent the untimely death.

Job experienced the most difficult grief in life—the
death of a child—times ten.

HE LOST HIS HEALTH

As if the loss of his possessions and children were not
difficult enough, Satan attacked Job one more time. He
claimed that Job was a selfish man who was only able to
go through his tragedy because he had not been touched
personally. Satan was wrong. Any loving father would
rather suffer himself than have his children hurt or lost
altogether. Job had already withstood the most difficult
test, but Satan insisted.

So Satan . . . afflicted Job with painful sores from the soles
of his feet to the top of his head. Then Job took a piece of
broken pottery and scraped himself with it as he sat among
the ashes.
Job 2:7, 8

A loss of health not only leads to discomfort and pain, but often to the loss of other important elements of life: freedom, recreation, perhaps even close friends. If you read through the book of Job, you discover what a mournful experience this loss of health was to Job.

- He had nightmares (7:14).
- Scabs formed over the sores and became black (30:28).
- His body was so disfigured that his appearance was revolting and his friends hardly recognized him (2:12).
- He experienced excessive weight loss (17:7).
- He had a severe fever (30:30).
- He felt pain day and night (30:17).

Everything Job had was taken from him—his wealth, his children, and now even his health. He had reason to grieve. He said:

> *"May the day of my birth perish,*
> *and the night it was said, 'A boy is born!'. . .*
> *Why did I not perish at birth,*
> *and die as I came from the womb?. . .*
> *For now I would be lying down in peace;*
> *I would be asleep and at rest. . .*
> *Why is light given to those in misery,*
> *and life to the bitter of soul. . . ?*
> *For sighing comes to me instead of food;*
> *my groans pour out like water.*
> *What I feared has come upon me;*
> *what I dreaded has happened to me.*
> *I have no peace, no quietness;*
> *I have no rest, but only turmoil."*   *Job 3:3-26*

In his grief, Job questioned God. But he did not abandon God. He still knew where to turn for comfort and answers to his questions. He knew that even in times of intense grief God's promises would still ring true.

PROMISES TO THOSE WHO GRIEVE

C. S. Lewis, the brilliant Christian author, was a bachelor until the middle of his life. Then he found what he described as near ecstatic happiness and a feeling of completion in his brief marriage to a woman who died of cancer a few years later. In his book, *A Grief Observed,* he poured out his anguish over her death and asked why God had given her to him, only to take her away so quickly. Lewis published this book under a pseudonym, perhaps fearing that it would seem out of character for a man with strong faith, who had helped others through their doubts about God, to write so honestly about his grief.

Grief is a trial even for a mature Christian like C. S. Lewis. But when those times come, we can take comfort in knowing God's promises to those who grieve.

GRIEF IS INEVITABLE

[There is] a time to weep and a time to laugh,
a time to mourn and a time to dance.   Ecclesiastes 3:4, 5

In several chapters we have discussed this point. Trials are going to come. Sickness, tragedies, and losses will occasionally invade your life.

Those who have studied the grief process relate that there is a normal cycle of grief when we experience a loss.

1. Shock. At first you are stunned by the news and don't know how to react. It all seems unreal. Sometimes when I visit a funeral home, the family of the deceased appears to be handling things well. Usually they are in shock. The reality has yet to sink in.

2. Denial. When the shock wears off, a grieving person goes through denial. The person who has lost a loved one might say, "This is not really happening. It's a nightmare that will be over soon. I keep thinking he will walk through the door any minute."

3. Anger. As reality begins to sink in, you might be tempted to get angry at the doctors for not doing more, or at the person who was driving who caused the accident. A person might even feel bitterness toward God for not preventing the tragedy. Job's wife told Job he should just go ahead and curse God and die.

4. Depression. In the cycle of grief, anger is often followed by prolonged periods of depression. The sorrow is not as intense as the first feelings of grief, and at times you may not even realize why you are depressed. Then there will be times when the memories come back and the sorrow is intensified. One day you are restless, the next day you're apathetic, then the next day you feel lonely or envious of others' happiness. During the first year of intense grief, each holiday or important date will bring memories and pain—your first Christmas alone, your first Easter, the first birthday, the first anniversary without your mate.

5. Acceptance. Some say the mourning process takes as long as two years. A friend of mine told me his second Christmas without his wife was more difficult than the first. His wife had died near Thanksgiving. During the first Christmas season he had many friends watching out for him, keeping him busy and encouraging him. The next Christmas he was caught off guard. It had been over a year since she had died, so he felt more confident he could handle things. He didn't plan as many activities to help him deal with his grief, and he was blindsided with memories of past Christmases with his wife. The Christmas Eve service with his two children was nearly more than he could endure.

Yet the final stage will come in time when you slowly, painfully begin to accept the loss as part of your life and return to normal existence. Life is never the same. There are changes and adjustments, and the loss is always there. But life does resume and become worthwhile again.

GOD WILL COMFORT YOU

When those times of grief come, as they inevitably will, we must remember that Job's friends were wrong. They told Job that he must have committed some sin to deserve all he was going through. Job's wife tried to get him to give in to his bitterness and just curse God and die. She must have felt as if life could never return to normal anyway and eternity without God couldn't be as bad as the pain of the present. She was wrong.

Job hadn't committed some sin for which God was punishing him. Grief is an inevitable part of life, no matter how faithful we are to God. Job's life would return to some form of normalcy in time, with the help of God. Though he mourned and wept and even questioned God, he did not reject God. He prayed and searched for answers. And God did come to him.

Job asked, "Lord, why did you even let me be born if you knew I would have to experience all this pain?" God could have angrily rejected Job for having the nerve to question Him. But the Lord was patient with Job. He not only answered his prayers, He comforted Job and rewarded his faithfulness.

The Lord blessed the latter part of Job's life more than the first. He had fourteen thousand sheep, six thousand camels, a thousand yoke of oxen and a thousand donkeys. And he also

had seven sons and three daughters. . . . Nowhere in all the
land were there found women as beautiful as Job's daughters,
and their father granted them an inheritance along with their
brothers. *Job 42:12, 13, 15*

God returned to Job all his wealth—twice as much as
he had before the tragedy—and gave him ten additional
children. Did you ever wonder why God didn't give Job
twice as many children? Some might say, "Because twenty
children are not a blessing!" No—because Job would have
twenty children in Heaven. His first ten had only tem-
porarily been taken from him.

The Bible promises that God will comfort us as well in
our times of grief.

Praise be to the God and Father of our Lord Jesus Christ, the
Father of compassion and the God of all comfort, who com-
forts us in all our troubles, so that we can comfort those in
any trouble with the comfort we ourselves have received from
God. *2 Corinthians 1:3, 4*

You might say, "I could never go through that. I
couldn't hold up under all that sorrow." But someone
said that we often overestimate our ability to handle
temptations and underestimate our ability to handle
trials. We think we can handle temptations that we have
no business going near, and Satan burns us. Then we
convince ourselves we could never bear up under certain
trials, until one day we are forced to do so, and we learn
quickly to depend on the Lord to help us make it
through our grief.

Jesus said, "Blessed are those who mourn, for they will
be comforted" (Matthew 5:4). Then He promised us the
Holy Spirit, who will comfort us in times of trouble.

And I will ask the Father, and he will give you another
Counselor to be with you forever—the Spirit of truth. The

world cannot accept him, because it neither sees him nor knows him. But you know him, for he lives with you and will be in you.   *John 14:16, 17*

Isaiah prophesied about the coming Messiah:

The Spirit of the Sovereign Lord is on me,
   because the Lord has anointed me
   to preach good news to the poor.
He has sent me to bind up the brokenhearted,
   to proclaim freedom for the captives
   and release for the prisoners,
to proclaim the year of the Lord's favor
   and the day of vengeance of our God,
to comfort all who mourn,
   and provide for those who grieve in Zion—
to bestow on them a crown of beauty
   instead of ashes,
the oil of gladness
   instead of mourning,
and a garment of praise
   instead of a spirit of despair.   *Isaiah 61:1-3*

I once delivered the eulogy at the funeral of a seven-year-old boy. I did the best I could to bring comfort and hope from the Word of God. His mother thanked me afterward and said, "If words could help, you couldn't have helped any more." I understood. Sometimes you can hurt so much that all the reminders of the reunion we will someday experience do not ease the pain. You need someone who will just be there.

When trouble comes your soul to try
You love the friend who just stands by.
Perhaps there's nothing he can do;
The thing is strictly up to you,
For there are troubles all your own;

And paths the soul must tread alone;
Times when love can't smooth the road,
Nor friendship lift the heavy load.
But just to feel you have a friend,
Who will stand by until the end;
Whose sympathy through all endures,
Whose warm handclasp is always yours,
It helps somehow to pull you through,
Although there's nothing he can do;
And so with fervent heart we cry,
"God bless the friend who just stands by."
("The Friend Who Just Stands By," Bertye Williams.)

The Holy Spirit can provide that kind of friendship and comfort. Paul wrote:

In the same way, the Spirit helps us in our weakness. We do not know what we ought to pray for, but the Spirit himself intercedes for us with groans that words cannot express.
Romans 8:26

The kind of honesty that Job and C. S. Lewis expressed does not drive us from God; it brings us nearer to Him. We have a Spirit that interprets for us with groans and utterances that we cannot understand. God loves us and hurts when we hurt. He has promised to comfort us, though the comforting process may take a while.

Cast all your anxiety on him because he cares for you.
1 Peter 5:7

LIFE IS SHORT

The period of grief can seem like forever. The moments crawl by and you are convinced the pain will never go away. But the Bible promises that this life, no matter how painful, compared to the span of eternity will seem very brief. The brevity of life is compared to

- a shadow (1 Chronicles 29:15).
- a swift runner (Job 9:25).
- the length of a handbreadth (Psalm 39:5).
- a vanishing mist (James 4:14).

There is waiting for you a time of eternity that will dwarf the brief time of pain you have experienced in this life. For those who walk with Christ, eternity is full of joy and reunions.

The ransomed of the Lord will return,
  They will enter Zion with singing;
  everlasting joy will crown their heads.
Gladness and joy will overtake them,
  and sorrow and sighing will flee away.   *Isaiah 51:11*

Billy Graham's grandfather Ben had lost an eye and a leg in the civil war. He lived a full life and died a few years before his wife. When Billy Graham's grandmother was dying, she said, "I see Jesus." Then she said, "Why, there's Ben, and he's got two legs and two eyes."

No matter what has caused your grief, remember that God is not punishing you. He loves you and is there to comfort you. And one day we will see Him face to face, where our time of grief will indeed turn to joy for eternity.

He will wipe every tear from their eyes. There will be no more death or mourning or crying or pain, for the old order of things has passed away.   *Revelation 21:4*

May our Lord Jesus Christ himself and God our Father, who loved us and by his grace gave us eternal encouragement and good hope, encourage your hearts and strengthen you in every good deed and word.   *2 Thessalonians 2:16, 17*

Precious in the sight of the Lord
  is the death of his saints.   *Psalm 116:15*

WHEN FACING DEATH

2 Timothy 4:6-8

Golf professional Paul Azinger had just won the 1993 PGA Championship and had ten tournament victories to his credit when he discovered he had cancer. His entire perspective on life was about to be radically changed. He wrote, "The next thing I know, I'm in an x-ray room lying on an ice cold table—shivering from nervousness. It was an awful feeling. As I lay there while the technician adjusted the machines, a genuine feeling of fear came upon me—I could die from cancer. But then another reality hit me even harder—I'm going to die eventually anyway. Whether from cancer or something else, I definitely going to die. It's just a question of when.

"In that same moment, something Larry Moody, the man who leads our Bible study on the PGA Tour, had said to me many times came to mind, 'Zinger, we're not in the land of the living going to the land of the dying. We're in the land of the dying going to the land of the living.'

"My major championship, my ten victories before that, everything I had accomplished in golf became meaningless to me." ("Links Letter," Vol. 15, No. 1, 1995, 800-9-0-LINKS).

The apostle Paul was facing death when he wrote:

For I am already being poured out like a drink offering, and the time has come for my departure. I have fought the good fight, I have finished the race, I have kept the faith. Now there is in store for me the crown of righteousness, which the Lord, the righteous Judge, will award to me on that day—and not only to me, but also to all who have longed for his appearing.   *2 Timothy 4:6-8*

You will die someday. Are you ready? Most people would rather not talk about it. Others bury their fear in a strange fascination with death. College students can now take classes on death and dying. The classes are among the most popular on campus. Educators are saying death has come out of the closet and into the classroom. Students are visiting morgues and making their own funeral arrangements.

Then there are movies and shows that constantly plot people on the brink of disaster. Our society's sick desire to see death fueled the making of a repulsive movie, "Faces of Death," which is nothing but real footage of people dying. One writer called America's fascination a "voyeurism of death."

Both extremes—nervous silence and constant obsession—are indications that the fear of death holds people in its grip.

There is also a lot of talk today about what happens to your spirit when you die. Will it be like the movie "Field of Dreams," where baseball players appear out of an Iowa cornfield to enjoy America's favorite pastime again? Will it be a series of unpredictable reincarnations like the New Agers and Eastern religions believe?

One man who was reading a Shirley MacLaine book asked his wife, "If reincarnation is true, does that mean I could come back in the next life as a worm?"

His wife quipped, "Oh, no, I've read that you can never be the same thing twice!"

For Christians, God's promises are clear. The writer of Hebrews wrote that Jesus came to destroy the devil, the one "who holds the power of death," and to "free those who all their lives were held in slavery by their fear of death" (Hebrews 2:14, 15). If you are a believer in Christ, you can face death with confidence, knowing that the following five things will happen to you when you die.

YOU WILL RECEIVE COMFORT

"It's not the dying I'm afraid of, it's the events leading up to the dying part." Have you ever thought that? It helps to remember that God is with us through whatever difficult circumstances might preclude our death.

Even though I walk
through the valley of the shadow of death,
I will fear no evil,
for you are with me;
your rod and your staff,
they comfort me.   *Psalm 23:4*

When I was a young boy, I would occasionally get a ride home from Little League baseball practice after dark. Often the driver would let me out at the dirt road that led the half-mile to our home. As I rode home, I would begin dreading that walk in the dark. I knew a robber or a wild animal was going to jump out of the bushes. I would sit in nervous silence during the ride, knowing I would run as fast as possible the entire half-mile home. But sometimes when we got to that dirt road, my father would be waiting for me. I would be so glad to see him! I would jump in his car and ride home in safety. All my fears had been for nothing.

I think the death experience will be like that. We anticipate how bad it will be, and we dread the thought of dying. But when we get there, the Father is waiting to take us home. He will comfort us through the "valley of the shadow of death." We will be perfectly safe, with nothing to fear.

YOUR SPIRIT WILL DEPART FROM YOUR BODY

Just before He died, Jesus said, "Father, into your hands I commit my spirit" (Luke 23:46). Jesus' body was buried in a tomb, but His spirit was not there.

Paul referred to death as being "away from the body" (2 Corinthians 5:8). In another Scripture, Paul called his death a "departure," using a nautical term that pictured a ship sailing out to sea (2 Timothy 4:6).

Your body is just an outer casing for the real you—your spirit. You can have your arms and legs amputated and your appendix, tonsils, and gall bladder removed, and you are still the same person. You can even have a heart transplant, but you are still "you" because there is a spirit inside of you that determines who you are. Just as a hand animates a glove, it is the spirit that energizes a body. When the spirit departs, the body, like a lifeless glove, is thrown aside.

YOU WILL BE IN THE PRESENCE OF THE LORD

The New Age, Eastern, and pagan philosophies about the spirit world have become very popular in our culture. There is a fascination with reincarnation, ghosts, spirits, and contacting the dead. The Bible forbids us to partake in such! As Christians, we have a greater promise. When you die, your spirit does not float around waiting for someone or something else to inhabit. It is not punished by having to wander the earth or go to a temporary place of purifying. Your spirit goes immediately to be with the Lord.

- Paul said that to be away from the body was to be "at home with the Lord" (2 Corinthians 5:8).

- When Jesus died, He prayed, "Father, into your hands I commit my spirit" (Luke 23:46).
- Stephen, when he was stoned to death, looked toward heaven and said, "Lord Jesus, receive my spirit" (Acts 7:59).
- In Luke 16 Jesus told a parable about a beggar named Lazarus who died and was immediately comforted at "Abraham's side" (Luke 16:22).

When my father died in February of 1995, there was too much snow and wind in Conneautville, Pennsylvania, to have a funeral procession and a graveside service. The funeral director said, "After the funeral, I'll take the body to the grave."

I felt like something was going to be left undone if I didn't see my father buried, so I said, "I'd like to go with you." After the funeral service I got my two sons, my brother and his son, and my sister's son Paul—six of us in all—and we followed the hearse to the cemetery in a four-wheel-drive vehicle.

We took my dad's casket and trudged about sixty yards through ten inches of blowing snow to the grave site. We watched as the grave diggers lowered the body into the grave. As we turned to leave, I said, "Let's have a prayer." It was like a scene out of "Shenandoah." We huddled with our arms around each other, and I began, "Oh God, this is such a cold and lonely place." I got choked up and had to finish in a whisper, "But I thank You that Your Word teaches that Dad's not in that body; he's with You in the warmth of Your arms. We know that to be absent from the body is to be present with the Lord."

There are many fascinating reports of Christians saying near their death, "I see Jesus!" or "I'm coming!" or "I see angels!" When my hometown preacher's wife, Mrs. D. P. Schaffer, died several years ago, she got out of her chair, looked up and said, "I'm coming." Then she slumped down, dead.

Lee Carter Maynard, a great preacher I knew, died when he was in his nineties. Just before he died, he said, "I see it! Do you see it? It's beautiful!"

I told a few of those stories in a revival meeting once. A woman came to me afterward and said, "I want to tell you what my uncle said when he died. He was not a Christian. He had lived a rebellious, horrible life. Just before he died, he got the most horrible look in his eyes and said, 'I see a fiery pit!'" What a dramatic reminder that the promises we are considering are only true for those who have been saved through Jesus Christ!

YOU WILL BE GIVEN A PERFECT BODY

There is an old story about two hillbillies and their son who had never visited the city. They came to town for the first time and saw the biggest building they had ever seen. The father said, "Ma, wait here. Me and junior will go check it out."

They went inside and saw the doors of an elevator open. They had never seen an elevator before. In stepped a shabbily-dressed old lady. The doors closed, the lights blinked, and bells whistled. When the doors opened again, out stepped a beautiful young woman. The old hillbilly said, "Son, go get your ma!"

One of the most exciting promises God gives us is that we will someday receive a new, glorified body. Jesus said, "Do not be amazed at this, for a time is coming when all who are in their graves will hear his voice and come out—those who have done good will rise to live, and those who have done evil will rise to be condemned" (John 5:28, 29). Consider these revealing words from Paul:

Brothers, we do not want you to be ignorant about those who fall asleep, or to grieve like the rest of men, who have no hope. We believe that Jesus died and rose again and so we be-

lieve that God will bring with Jesus those who have fallen asleep in him. According to the Lord's own word, we tell you that we who are still alive, who are left till the coming of the Lord, will certainly not precede those who have fallen asleep. For the Lord himself will come down from heaven, with a loud command, with the voice of the archangel and with the trumpet call of God, and the dead in Christ will rise first. After that, we who are still alive and are left will be caught up together with them in the clouds to meet the Lord in the air. And so we will be with the Lord forever.

1 Thessalonians 4:13-17

How can we say that "to be absent from the body is to be present with the Lord" and also say that the bodies of the saints are going to rise when Christ returns? How can God "bring with Jesus those who have fallen asleep" and then those same people rise from the grave?

We can understand that Scripture if we remember that we will follow the pattern of Christ. When Jesus died on the cross, His body was placed in a tomb, but His spirit was not there. His spirit returned to the body three days later when it was brought back to life.

So it is with His followers. When we die, our spirits go to be with the Lord. We will not yet have our perfect eternal bodies. We will still be alert, full of joy and personality, and able to communicate with the Creator. But it is not until Christ's return that our bodies will be resurrected and perfected so that we can inhabit them once again. Our bodies will be miraculously raised and will meet our spirits in the air! That is one of the reasons Christ's return will be such a spectacular sight!

In the past, Christians insisted that their bodies be buried facing the east. They believed Jesus was going to return in the eastern sky, and they wanted to be resurrected facing the east. Today we are so carnal minded that we insist on a watertight casket or a sealed crypt. I have decided I want a flip-top box, so I can come out of there quickly!

A skeptic will say, "That is all too supernatural to believe. It's too fanciful." But if you had never seen a human baby born, would you believe it if someone described it to you? Would you believe that a sperm and an egg smaller than the eye can see, destined to die if left by themselves, could be miraculously joined to become the first cell of a human body? And that the cells would continue to multiply inside the woman until a perfectly formed human baby came out? You would say that is too fanciful to believe. But God performs that miracle every day. Is it that difficult to believe He could return our souls to resurrected bodies? Paul wrote:

But someone may ask, "How are the dead raised? With what kind of body will they come?" How foolish! What you sow does not come to life unless it dies. When you sow, you do not plant the body that will be, but just a seed, perhaps of wheat or something else. But God gives it a body as he has determined, and to each kind of seed he gives its own body. . . .

So will it be with the resurrection of the dead. The body that is sown is perishable, it is raised imperishable; it is sown in dishonor, it is raised in glory; it is sown in weakness, it is raised in power; it is sown a natural body, it is raised a spiritual body. . . .

Listen, I tell you a mystery: We will not all sleep, but we will all be changed—in a flash, in the twinkling of an eye, at the last trumpet. For the trumpet will sound, the dead will be raised imperishable, and we will be changed. For the perishable must clothe itself with the imperishable, and the mortal with immortality."

1 Corinthians 15:35-38, 42-44, 51-53

The body you receive will be a perfect body. Aren't you

glad? If you are eighty years old, and you have arthritis and a hearing aid, you will not want to pick up where you left off when you get your body back. If you're five feet tall and overweight, or six-feet-five and skinny, you are probably hoping for some improvement when you get your glorified body. I heard about a choir cantata where the women sang, "We'll have new bodies," and the men responded, "Praise the Lord!"

YOU WILL INHERIT A HEAVENLY HOME

"Do not let your hearts be troubled. Trust in God; trust also in me. In my Father's house are many rooms; if it were not so, I would have told you. I am going there to prepare a place for you. And if I go and prepare a place for you, I will come back and take you to be with me that you also may be where I am."   *John 14:1-3*

People have some strange views of Heaven. The traditional thought of sitting on clouds all day strumming harps is not very accurate. The things we read in Scripture about our eternal home are very exciting. Heaven is described as a place where there is no crying, no pain, no sorrow, no death (see Revelation 21:4).

Scripture speaks of the wedding supper of the Lamb (Revelation 19:9), where we will feast together. Think about eating in a perfect place. You don't have to worry about fat grams, cholesterol, or your blood pressure; "guilt-free" ice cream will not be necessary, because there will be no guilt! Weight Watchers will be out of business!

Jesus said there would be "many rooms" in His Father's house. I picture an "instant replay room" where you can review any event in history exactly as it happened. Then maybe you can visit a "question and answer room," where you can learn the answers to all the difficult and troubling questions on earth. I hope there is an "instructional room," where you can learn how to do things you did not have time to do on earth: photography, flying, skiing, painting.

We may not know exactly what Heaven is going to be like, but we can remember the happiest, most fulfilling moments we have experienced on this earth—the prettiest place we have ever visited, the best friends we have ever had, the best meals we have eaten, the most exciting times of worship; Heaven will be infinitely more perfect, more enjoyable, and more fulfilling than those experiences.

I think if Jesus fished after He was raised from the dead, then I will be able to play golf in Heaven—on the prettiest courses you can imagine. The Bible actually speaks of a new Heaven and a new earth, and it seems we will be able to travel from one to the other (Revelation 21:1). One poet described it like this:

The view of Heaven that I sing
Is not of angels on the wing,
White robed, with harps and golden crowns.
I vision rather little towns,
With smogless skies and rivers clear
And not an airplane you can hear.
No dust, no rust, no rats, no rot,
No raucous rock, no potent pot,
No growing old with weakened sight,
No dentures slipping when you bite,
No bombs, no guns, no courts, no jails,
Where all succeed and no one fails,
No strikes, no layoffs, full employment,
And everyone with job enjoyment.
All tell the truth, state only facts,
No wars, no debt, no income tax.
According to this dream of mine,
In Heaven no one stands in line

And there are only smiling faces
And lots and lots of parking places.
                    (source unknown)

The apostle John saw a vision of Heaven. He described it this way:

Then I saw a new heaven and a new earth, for the first heaven and the first earth had passed away, and there was no longer any sea. I saw the Holy City, the new Jerusalem, coming down out of heaven from God, prepared as a bride beautifully dressed for her husband. And I heard a loud voice from the throne saying, 'Now the dwelling of God is with men, and he will live with them. They will be his people, and God himself will be with them and be their God. He will wipe every tear from their eyes. There will be no more death or mourning or crying or pain, for the old order of things has passed away."

He who was seated on the throne said, "I am making everything new!" Then he said, "Write this down, for these words are trustworthy and true." Revelation 21:1-5

The Bible says we will be able to recognize Abraham, Isaac, and Jacob at the feast (see Luke 13:28, 29). I think that means we will be able to recognize one another, too. Paul said, "Then I shall know fully, even as I am fully known" (1 Corinthians 13:12). To me, this is the greatest part of Heaven—spending eternity with Jesus Christ and being reunited with the ones we love.

A few years ago Judy and I returned to Louisville after a two-week mission trip overseas. We were very glad to be home. When we walked up the tunnel from the plane into the airport, there were about seventy-five people who had come to greet us. They cheered and embraced us. It felt good to be welcomed home.

I think Heaven will be like that. I picture an "arrival

board" where my friends and loved ones who have gone on before me can see exactly when I will be arriving. Then they will gather to meet me, just after I meet Jesus.

I picture them applauding when I arrive. My dad will be there—not first in line, because he would never see himself as that important—but he will be the first one I look for. Can you imagine the embraces, the tears of joy, the laughter that awaits you?

> *Friends will be there I have loved long ago,*
> *Joy like a river around me will flow,*
> *Yet just a smile from my Savior I know,*
> *Will through the ages be glory for me.*
> ("O That Will Be Glory," Charles H. Gabriel.)

Paul Azinger recovered from his chemotherapy and returned to the PGA tour. He has done very well. But that bout with cancer deepened his perspective. He wrote, "I've made a lot of money since I've been on the tour and I've won a lot of tournaments. That happiness is always temporary. The only way you will ever have true contentment is in a personal relationship with Jesus Christ. I'm not saying that nothing ever bothers me and I don't have problems, but I feel like I've found the answer to the six-foot hole. I know I'll spend eternity with God. And I have a promise that as a child of God, He'll help me deal with anything. He promises to give me contentment no matter what life brings—even cancer.

"God did not intend this world to be the best of all possible places. But it's a place where we can prepare for the best of all possible places."